THE HOWELL BOOK OF PUPPY RAISING

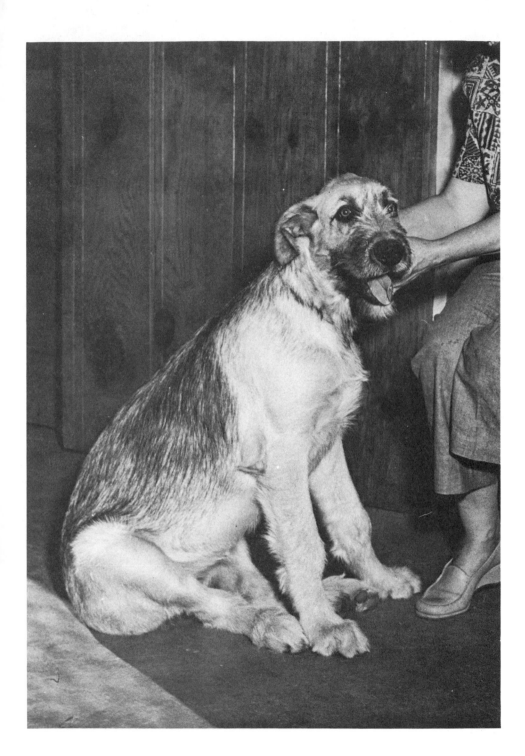

The Howell Book of
PUPPY RAISING

by Charlotte Schwartz

First Edition

HOWELL
BOOK HOUSE
New York

Howell Book House
Macmillan Publishing Company
866 Third Avenue, New York, NY 10022
Collier Macmillan Canada, Inc.

Library of Congress Cataloging-in-Publication Data

Schwartz, Charlotte.
  The Howell book of puppy raising.

  Bibliography: p. 170
  Summary: Discusses the birth, growth, and development of
puppies, how to care for them, and how best to acclimate them to
human family life.
  1. Dogs. 2. Puppies. [1. Dogs] I. Howell Book
House. II. Title
SF427.S365   1987   636.7′0887   86-27851
ISBN 0-87605-770-9

Macmillan books are available at special discounts for bulk purchases
for sales promotions, premiums, fund-raising, or educational use.
For details, contact:

              Special Sales Director
              Macmillan Publishing Company
              866 Third Avenue
              New York, NY 10022

10 9 8 7 6 5

Printed in the United States of America

This book is dedicated to

BONNIE and ANGEL

*Another lifetime with them
couldn't possibly return all
the love and companionship
they gave to me.*

Poodles are among the breeds that often show a dilution factor in their color. The light face and paws of the puppy at the right indicate it will clear to a silver compared to its black littermate.
—*Evelyn M. Shafer*

The Golden Retriever is a superb gundog, yet many thousands never are called upon to perform the breed's work. Goldens adapt very well to a variety of roles and make excellent companions for dog owners with greatly varying needs.

Contents

Introduction: A Canine Crystal Ball   **9**

Chapter 1   Genetics: Choosing the Best Parents   **15**

Genetic History . . . Parents: *Temperament, Physical Health,
Mental Health, Conformation, Specific Breed Traits, Environment*
. . . Mixed Breeds . . . Puppy Sources . . . Conclusion

Chapter 2   In Utero Environment   **35**

Age of Dam . . . Physical Condition of Dam . . . Management of
Mating . . . Management of Dam . . . Feeding for Optimum
Breeding. . . Exercise. . . Housing. . . Activities. . . Emotional
Factors . . . Whelping Experience

Chapter 3   Birth Environment: Birth to 20 Days   **54**

Neonatal Period . . . Transition Period . . . Environmental Tem-
perature. . . Care and Nutrition of the Dam . . . Nutrition During
Lactation . . . Dam's Care of the Puppies . . . Housing . . .
Cleanliness . . . Comfort . . . Litter Size . . . Interaction with
Dam, Sire, Other Animals. . . Interaction with Humans. . . Litter
Socialization . . . Early Nerve and Muscle Development . . .
SPECIAL PUPPIES: Sick Puppies, The One-Puppy Litter, Or-
phaned Puppies, Temperature Control, Housing, Evacuation, Feed-
ing Orphan Puppies

Chapter 4   Litter Socialization Period: 21 to 35 Days   **84**

The Senses . . . Awareness . . . Interaction with the Pack . . .
Eating Habits: *Weaning Procedure* . . . Interaction with Humans

Chapter 5   Human Socialization Period: Weeks Five to Twelve   97

Declaration of Independence and a First Fear Period . . . Socialization and Chewing on People . . . Order of Dominance . . . "Every Dog Needs a Number" (Dominance Down Instructions) . . . Experiences . . . Puppy Testing . . . Puppy Aptitude Tests . . . Early Training: *Housetraining and Crate Training* . . . Seven Steps to Crate Train a Puppy . . . Outdoor Runs and Kennels . . . More Play Learning . . . Veterinary Care and Immunizations

Chapter 6   New Home Environment: Weeks Seven to Twelve   127

A Fear Period . . . Feeding the New Puppy . . . Caring for the Puppy . . . Localization . . . Territoriality and Order of Dominance . . . Puppy Proofing Your Home . . . Early Schooling: *Lead training, Come, Sit, Down* . . . Keeping Your Puppy Well Groomed . . . Play

Chapter 7   Juvenile Period: Twelve Weeks to Six Months   149

Teething . . . Another Fear Period . . . Sexual Development and Neutering

Chapter 8   You, The New Owner   155

The Purpose of Acquiring a Dog . . . Lifestyles . . . Choosing the Right Breed . . . Cost and Commitment . . . Your Present Skills, Effort, and Patience . . . Training and Your Attitude About It . . . Specialized Training

Chapter 9   In the Final Analysis   164

Conclusion

Breeds of Dogs   167

Bibliography   170

Puppy Development Chart   172

Introduction: A Canine Crystal Ball

EXACTLY WHAT is a canine crystal ball anyway? The dictionary defines a crystal ball as a globe-shaped crystal used for forecasting the future. Back in the 1960s I decided that a literary canine crystal ball might be useful to people, like myself, who wanted or needed to know more about dogs and how they develop. I knew instinctively that a finished product was only as good as the parts that went into making it, but I needed guidance.

The need for such a volume arose years ago when I began to breed and show Miniature Schnauzers and Airedales. Actually, I found many books on a wide variety of dog subjects and read them all. I also found what appeared to be very important information regarding genetics, whelping and raising dogs written by various experts in the field. I read this material, too, but found it extremely difficult to comprehend. Only after long hours of reading and rereading did I begin to understand the meaning of these reports. Even then, I often needed help from some veterinary friends.

During the twenty-five years since I began to study canine development, there has been a wealth of valuable information printed. There are now books on genetics, dog behavior, puppy development, dog training and a dozen more dog-related subjects. There are even books on how to buy dogs and many breeds have at least one book devoted solely to raising and living with that particular breed.

Of course, reading books doesn't necessarily answer all one's questions on a given subject. In those early days, I subscribed to many dog periodicals, searched libraries for books on related subjects such as wolves, psychology, physiology, ecology and collected information in bits and pieces from experienced dog people wherever I found them.

To delve more deeply into a particular area of interest, I attended seminars and clinics. Many of those I found most frustrating because the experts presented papers that were academically oriented rather than appropriate for the average fancier. I recall attending a seminar at which six eminent veterinary authorities presented important findings on such subjects as torsion and bloat, hereditary canine diseases, dental problems in dogs and canine nutrition. When the day ended, I remember commenting to a friend that, of the six papers presented, I understood only one of them!

Fortunately, the audience received copies of all the papers given that day. But it took me months to transcribe the medical language into a usable form so that I, a lay person and dog breeder, could use the information we'd received.

What I needed back then (and could still use today) was an encyclopedic volume on puppies and why they grow up the way they do. It would have made my job of breeding, training, showing and living with dogs much easier and more satisfying—and much more pleasant for the dogs!

In this book I've approached the subject of puppies in a chronological order—from the initial idea to life with an ideal companion. After all, a dog is made of many things, not the least of which are the genes that went into creating it in the first place. And I'm not speaking of only its parents for they, too, brought many genes from their ancestors to the mating.

It is generally accepted that behavior—the way a living being reacts to a stimulus—is caused by one or more of the following factors: genetics, environment and reflexes. A dog's ability or inability to adapt to its environment is, therefore, directly related to these factors. Consequently, I've divided the critical periods in a puppy's life into chapters and address each one separately to show how one or more of these factors play an important role in canine development. For example, in Chapters 3, 4 and 5 I discuss canine interaction with humans. These discussions are not repeats of one another, but are distinct descriptions of how interaction with humans at different stages in a puppy's development can have lasting effects on the puppy.

To help clarify the whole matter of development and what happens when, I've created a *Puppy Development Chart* (see page 172). With it the reader can pinpoint exactly what's happening to a puppy in every area of growth during any given timeframe—from the day of birth until complete maturity. I would have loved to have this chart back when I started breeding dogs, but it didn't exist then. Now it does, and it can be used for ready reference once the contents of the book have been digested.

I've tried not to assume anything, so that even a beginning fancier will not get lost along the way, as I did many years ago. Such infrequently discussed subjects as the mental health of the pregnant bitch, the size of the litter and the types of toys a puppy plays with are examined. Finally, I've taken the technical side of canine development and simplified it without changing the meaning so that everyone can easily understand the valuable information that our scientists have learned and shared with us.

Who, then, can use this book? If you can answer "Yes" to at least one of the questions below, then this book—my canine crystal ball—can help you. Regardless of your area of interest, this book is written to help you be more objective in your interactions with dogs in general and puppies in particular.

- Do you own or intend to buy a puppy for a pet?
- Do you breed dogs?
- Do you train dogs and/or puppies?
- Do you sell dogs and puppies?
- Do you board dogs and/or puppies?
- Do you groom dogs?
- Do you show dogs?
- Do you care for dogs and/or puppies for others?
- Do you instruct people in dog obedience or any other specialized field of dog behavior?
- Do you just like puppies and want to learn more about them?

In short, I wrote this book to help a wide range of people. I wrote it for people with puppies, for dog trainers, for breeders and would-be breeders and for just about anyone who has a need or desire to further their understanding of what goes into a puppy to make it the kind of dog it will become. There are many factors that constitute the building blocks of a dog and each breed of dog can and should carry the unique traits for which its breed was originally bred. Only through understanding all the aspects of canine development can we hope to perpetuate the qualities in each breed and enjoy man's most trusted companion.

Throughout the research and writing of this book, dozens of people offered opinions, gave me ideas, loaned me puppy photos and shared their experiences with me. To all of them, I say thank you. Each small bit added to the whole and made it all possible.

This introduction would be incomplete without mentioning the many people who spent months and years investigating the behavior and development of canines. People such as Michael Fox, Peter Messent, John Paul Scott and John L. Fuller, Clarence Pfaffenberger and David Mech and many, many more. Without their earlier investigations this book and the successful rearing of dogs would have been much more difficult.

There are a few special people who must be thanked publicly, for without them I never would have completed the task. The first is my grandson, Brett, who put his arm around my shoulders one day and said, "Just think of all the puppies and people you're going to help with this book, Grandma. It'll be terrific!"

To Nancy Brayton, Lois Wenner and Karla Martin I send a heartfelt "Thanks, Ladies!" My fellow instructors, they left me alone to write and read when I needed to be alone. They taught some of my classes and answered a hundred questions from students so I could pursue my writing.

Dr. Donald Collins gets a large portion of public thanks, too, for without his expertise in canine nutrition and his readable writing ability this book would surely be lacking. Dr. Collins is quite a fellow. He's more than a specialist in what kind of food a dog should eat. He's also aware of people in general and how they approach feeding their dogs. He knows, for example, that good canine nutrition originates from the owner and he talks to us in a language we can understand, tempering it with genuine concern for us and our dogs. Above all, he uses generous helpings of common sense in his approach to the subject. He writes clearly and concisely and explains the reasons behind his teachings. His own book, *The Collins' Guide to Dog Nutrition* (Howell Book House), should be in every dog owner's library—it carries on where this one ends in the course of a dog's life.

And finally, heartfelt thanks go to my best friend, Sue Hill, who kept saying, "You can do it!" when I'd falter and wonder aloud if I was the right person to write such a book. Her faith carried me through some difficult times and helped me get this book together.

As I said, I once looked for a canine crystal ball to help me forecast the future of the puppies I wanted to produce. Now, twenty-odd years and a lot of learning later, I've tried to write one.

The Retrieve Test determines the puppy's level of interest in moving objects and his desire to pick up and carry them. —*Charlotte Schwartz*

13

Just as individual breeds show typical physical traits, so do they display distinctive behavioral characteristics. The Irish Terrier is typical of the courageous, loyal terriers.

—*Evelyn M. Shafer*

14

1

Genetics: Choosing the Best Parents

THE STORY OF GENETICS is a fascinating one. Unfortunately, many people view it as a mysterious science that is almost impossible for the layman to understand. Words such as *chromosomes, Mendelian Law, dominant, recessive, zygote* and *heritability* add coals to the fire of confusion and further convince people that genetics is a discipline best left in the laboratory with the scientists.

One of the most fascinating things about the study of genetics is that its most basic work was performed—not in a laboratory by a research scientist—by Gregor Mendel, a Czechoslovakian clergyman and botany teacher. Back in the latter half of the 1800s, Mendel conducted some experiments with green peas in a little garden behind his church in the town of Brunn. Unsure of just what his experiments meant, he wrote about his findings and sent the report to a scientific magazine in 1866.

It wasn't until many years later, the early 1900s, that two doctors referred to Mendel's report and recognized its significance to humanity. Dr. L. H. Bailey of Cornell University and, later, Dr. Hugo DeVris of Holland realized that Mendel's findings provided the answer to the questions the world had been asking about heredity for ages. They called his findings Mendel's Law or the Laws of Mendelian Inheritance.

Mendel's Law of how genes affect inheritance applies in some measure to mammals, birds, fish and plant life. In fact, nearly all forms of life are governed by Mendel's Law. That's why it is so important to mankind. Mendel's Law, for example, is the factor behind why we are able to buy five pounds of potatoes all of approximately the same size, why all the roses from a particular strain look alike, why all the chicks from a specific bloodline grow up to be duplicates of one another, how we grow certain plants that produce the same elements for pharmaceutical use year after year, and why great race horses tend to beget great race horses.

Using Mendel's Law, man can breed better dogs more consistently and not by accident. By keeping the best traits of the parents, and through selective breeding over generations, man is also able to produce puppies with fewer faults and genetic abnormalities. Of course, the quality of the foundation stock, or the dogs with which a person begins a breeding program, will determine the quality of the puppies and their puppies' progeny through the generations that follow.

Of all the books I've read and lectures I've heard on inheritance, one of the most easily understood came at a seminar I attended many years ago. Dr. Braxton B. Sawyer, a noted hound breeder and clergyman from Fort Smith, Arkansas, presented a paper titled, "How the New Knowledge of Genetics Can Help Breed Better Dogs." In it, Dr. Sawyer explained the function of heredity and the basic principles of genetics.

Basically, Dr. Sawyer explained that the characteristics of a breed are not transmitted to the puppies through the blood. Instead, the reproductive germ cells of each dog, male and female, combine during breeding to produce a replica of the two individuals being mated.

The reproductive cell of the male has 78 chromosomes. The same is true for the female. The genes are found within these chromosomes. At breeding, one-half of the chromosomes of the male unite with one-half of the chromosomes of the female, thereby creating the individual puppy. Thus, each puppy receives one-half of its genes from its mother and one-half from its father. Whether the halves are good or bad genes cannot be determined until the puppy is born and matures.

Some of the genes of each parent are known as *dominant* genes and some are called *recessive*. Many factors go into determining

16

whether the specific dominant or recessive genes of a particular breeding are good or bad. Knowing what is meant by dominant and recessive genes, how they work toward creating the individual puppy and how humans can control the breeding of dogs to produce desired results or *heredity* is the study of genetics.

One of the best books on the subject, with explanations the layman can use, is *Genetics for Dog Breeders* by Frederick B. Hutt (W. H. Freeman & Co., 1979). Suffice it to say that when the spermatozoa of the male imbeds itself into the egg of the female a *zygote* is formed and we say a puppy has been conceived. From that moment on we cannot control the genetic makeup of the eventual dog. That's why understanding genetics is so important to those who would breed.

It seems obvious, then, that the study of genetics is not for the impatient, the person who wants answers yesterday. Rather, it is a complex discipline requiring a great deal of study and years of practical experience in the breeding of dogs to learn the results of inbreeding, line breeding and outbreeding of specific bloodlines in a given breed to see which traits are dominant, which are recessive, which dogs carry desirable genes and which carry undesirable (even lethal) ones. But it is not mysterious and can be mastered by the layman who is willing to study.

Just because a person is interested in obtaining a puppy, however, does not mean that he must become involved in years of research and study. It does mean that one should seek out those who have done just that for help in acquiring the best puppy for his needs. It goes without saying, the more knowledgeable one becomes about a subject, the more one will benefit from that knowledge.

Genetic History

As we have learned, the chromosomes are the containers or packages that contain the genes. There are 78 chromosomes, or 39 pairs, in each dog. The genes are what give the puppy its individual characteristics or traits (type of coat, color, ear set and the like). Genes also determine the predisposition of certain types of behaviors, such as dominance, submission and emotional stability, and most of the selective traits used by dogs to perform specific behaviors, such as hunting, scenting, pulling and racing.

When we study a puppy's genetic history we are looking not only at its parents but at its grandparents, great grandparents and earlier ancestors as well. Those individuals contributed their genes down through the generations and some of their genes can manifest themselves in the puppy. By using simple mathematics we can see that the closer an ancestor is to the puppy the greater the genetic influence will be on that puppy.

Consequently, it behooves the breeder to use a dam and sire each of which carries the highest percentage of desirable genes possible. After all, since breeding dogs carries a certain amount of luck with it, it seems just good sense to stack the deck in one's favor! That is why successful dog breeders have made a study of the genetic history of their own breeding stock. By determining in advance which dogs carry the traits most needed to perform a certain job or produce the best temperament or the most correct structure of all these traits combined, the breeder can select the dogs most suited for breeding in order to foster those traits and eliminate the undesirable ones.

Let's look at a typical example of the value of studying genetic history. Suppose I was going to obtain a German Shepherd Dog puppy that I intended to raise as a search and rescue dog. First, I'd list as many of the qualities of a good rescue dog that I could think of. Physical stamina, curiosity, self-confidence, friendliness, scenting ability and trainability would all be important qualities I'd be looking for in such a working dog.

Now let's assume I knew of a litter of German Shepherd Dog puppies for sale in my community. I would go to see them, meet the owners and the dam and talk to the owners about the sire if I couldn't see him as well.

Suppose, when I arrived at the home of the litter, I found the mother of the puppies out in the back yard barking at me through the fence. This behavior would seem only natural; after all, she recognized a stranger at the door and was alerting the owners inside that I was there.

However, once the owners invited me into the house and I sat in the living room chatting with them and they brought the bitch in to meet me, I would expect her to be at least mannerly and not fearful or threatening, especially if the puppies were in another room. Instead, however, suppose she came into the room, ran up to within a few feet of me, refused to make friends and eventually hid behind one of the owners. Further efforts on the owner's part failed to bring her around to a point where I could pet her or at least see her relax.

18

Discussion with the owners brought out the fact that the father of the puppies was a beautiful animal ("He has a long furry coat and a great bushy tail!") and that the sire's father is a bit overprotective around his home and has bitten several people who were guests in the owner's home.

"But we're sure the puppies will be fine," assured the owners. "After all, the mother hasn't bitten anyone—why, she's afraid of people and would never get close enough to bite anyone!"

The mother's behavior and the comments regarding both parents and the grandsire would tell me almost immediately that these puppies were not good candidates for search and rescue work. First, I would be very suspicious of the grandsire's "overprotectiveness"—it could be environmentally induced or hereditary. The territoriality trait is strongly inherited as opposed to some other traits that are only weakly influenced by heredity.

Secondly, the dam's shyness would not be suitable for a dog that needed an extraordinary amount of self-confidence, friendliness and courage, such as required for search work. Finally, the comment about the sire's "long, furry coat" would warn me that the puppies carried the genes for a long coat and the pup I chose might have one. A long, flowing coat may be beautiful to look at, but is not suitable for a dog that must work in brush, forest, open water, swamp and snow. Therefore, buying such a puppy as this would be foolish on my part (I'd spend more time keeping the dog's coat clean and free of debris than searching!).

Here's another, more common, example of why we should study the genetic history of a dog before embarking on a lifetime with it. A young couple with three small children, ages two through seven, wants to buy a dog for a family pet. They have friends who have a litter of Dachshund puppies for sale. They know in advance that the parents of the puppies are well bred and have been shown at local shows. Furthermore, the sire and dam are extremely intelligent. They hunt regularly with the husband on a large farm where they've been very successful at controlling the ground hog population. Surely, the couple reasons, the puppies will be as intelligent and beautiful as the parents.

Well, to make a long story short, the couple buys a female Dachshund puppy from the litter in question. Seven months go by before I get a phone call from the wife. The puppy, now nine months old, is a delightful animal in every way whenever the children are not around! But when the children are at home, which is most of the time since they have a two-year-old, the dog creates such chaos that they have to lock her in the laundry room where she howls and destroys whatever she can get her mouth around.

Following a long consultation, I have a pretty fair picture of what's happening in the household. The puppy is fine—alert, friendly, willing, intelligent and possessing a high excitability level. The same is true of the children. And therein lies the problem.

It is simply a matter of right dog, wrong family. The little Dachshund, due to her genetic history, is a working hunter. In short, she will go after anything that moves quickly. Picture, then, six little feet racing past you to the tune of childish squeals and you, an excitable Dachshund, grabbing at those flying feet with tiny sharp teeth!

"I thought a small dog would be perfect for us," cried the wife. "She's so good when things are quiet around the house. And we love her so much."

As frequently happens in cases like this, we did find a solution to the chaos. The family made appropriate adjustments so they could live in harmony with the dog and the Dachshund didn't have to spend most of her life in the laundry room. But it took a lot of patience, time and effort on the part of the couple to organize their growing family and their active little dog. And the whole experience could have been avoided if they had chosen a different dog, perhaps even a different breed.

Here's something else for you to think about. Suppose you were interested in a particular breed and you'd found a bloodline, or family, within that breed that appealed to you. Let's say the breed was a Golden Retriever and the bloodline was a working line. That is, many of the dogs from the genetic bloodline were working at hunting with their various owners and proving to be top quality field dogs.

You, on the other hand, were looking for a Golden Retriever as a family pet. You live in a city or suburban area and have no time or interest in hunting or field trial work. You are prepared to give the puppy adequate exercise within your own lifestyle, but the puppy will probably grow up never seeing a pheasant or hearing a gunshot.

Buying a puppy from this type of bloodline would more than likely create severe frustrations for you and the puppy. The dog, as an adult, would always have the instinct to run and hunt. You would always want to take leisurely walks in the park, spend whatever time you had with the dog in quiet contemplation or participate in some supervised play such as a game of fetch. Both of you, then, would always be wishing for something that neither of you could give to the other. Many times, I've seen people make that mistake only to have to end the relationship and find a more suitable home for the dog. And it was always sad and painful for both the owner and the dog. This is another reason why studying genetic history is so important and beneficial to both you and your prospective canine companion.

Parents

In addition to the genetic history of a puppy, there are other factors that should be considered before we can begin to predict the future of the puppy. Collectively, these and other factors can make all the difference in the world when it comes to getting a puppy off to the right start in life. We must remember that, in addition to genes, the parents of the puppy will influence the offspring in many other ways as well. Let's consider some of the more important ones.

Temperament

In Chapter 5 we will go into temperament and how to develop it in puppies, but in this chapter we are talking about the temperament of the parents exclusively. We must keep in mind that the temperaments of the parents have been formed long before they were bred.

It stands to reason that puppies will take on the temperament of the mother due to the intensity of their relationship at a most critical time in their lives. If the mother is nervous, neurotic or frightened she will pass on these traits to the puppies as she goes about interacting with them. On the other hand, if the dam is friendly, outgoing, self-assured and interested in her world, then her puppies will develop the same characteristics as they mimic her.

As we've seen in the example of the German Shepherd rescue dog, temperament can be hereditary. Most geneticists consider the tendency to be about 10 percent inherited, therefore a great deal of it can be controlled by environment. However, the predisposition will always be there, and only an experienced, knowledgeable person should consider raising a puppy from parents with undesirable temperament traits.

Again it is important to remember that here we are assessing the health of the parents at the time the prospective buyer first meets them, which is probably when the puppies are about six to eight weeks old. Parental health at the time they were bred is another matter we will take up in Chapter 2.

If one is lucky enough to see the sire, he should display good weight, a clean, healthy looking coat and an alertness that indicates his general interest in life. Although the person seeing the sire for the first time will probably not have the opportunity to observe his stool, the dog should have a normal appetite with well-formed stool. A few questions directed to the owner can usually determine the answers to these queries.

The dam's health, however, will be much more difficult to determine. First of all, if she nursed the puppies well, one may find her looking rather bedraggled to say the least. Her coat may be dull and quite thin. Her nipples will be hanging low beneath her belly and she may have lost a considerable amount of weight. In short, she may look like some poor creature at death's door from starvation and the elements.

Providing the puppies look and act healthy, the owners demonstrate an awareness and concern for her care at this critical time and she herself acts like she's feeling fit, there should be little worry. When a dam nurses and cares for a litter of puppies, say anywhere from six to 12 of them, every part of her being will be drained in the process. Because the puppies take so much from her, she will eat enormous amounts of food—up to three times her normal ration—and still not gain weight.

However, a few weeks free of the responsibility of raising puppies combined with good rehabilitative care should see her looking like her old self again. The actual weaning process is an individual affair. Some dams will nurse a litter of puppies for months if allowed. Others decide to wean the pups when they are barely three weeks old. Then, of course, the breeder may have definite plans for the weaning process and take the puppies away from the mother at a specific time. More often than not, breeders will apply a middle-of-the road regimen whereby the bitch will be allowed to nurse the pups at night and perhaps once during the day; the owners will offer commercial food to the puppies the rest of the time. This method seems to work rather well and prepares the puppies for the day when they will go to new homes.

There is one other area of physical health we need to emphasize here. That is the necessity of having the parents be free of hereditary abnormalities that can be so serious as to impair the health of the puppies at a future time in their lives. Unfortunately, most of these abnormalities are highly hereditary (25 to 40 percent), thus making them a definite consideration for the prospective puppy owner. For example, hip dysplasia is often found in many large breeds and is extremely hereditary. For this reason the parents should have been X-rayed and pronounced free of it. Severe hip dysplasia can cause lameness and a great deal of suffering in dogs of all ages. Furthermore, dysplastic dogs frequently suffer painful and debilitating arthritis as they get older.

Such other abnormalities as hemophilia, epilepsy (which can manifest itself in dogs at about two years of age) and eye disorders, such as progressive retinal atrophy, are all problems about which one should become aware. It is important to remember that these and many other abnormalities are inherited, and it is almost impossible to determine whether or not puppies have any of these just by looking at them. Therefore, one must question the litter owners to determine if the parents have any hereditary abnormalities.

Finally, it is the breeder's responsibility to ensure that the dam was free of internal parasites before and during her pregnancy. This is a matter not to be taken lightly. Having a healthy dam to produce and raise healthy puppies is like having a fine strong box to protect your finest jewels. How can the contents be safe if the package is falling apart?

Mental Health

An adult dog of sound mind and stable emotions can cope with the world it lives in. Similarly, it will contribute a great deal to the emotional foundation of its progeny. It seems reasonable to assume that dogs who are "solid citizens" will influence their offspring by developing, within the puppies during that critical period in their lives, the soundness of mind and emotions that they can use when they begin learning to cope in their own worlds as mature dogs.

Likewise, mental handicaps—from neurosis to extreme disturbances—will affect the puppies in an equally strong manner. And, like the physical being that produced the puppies, the mental state of that being is equally important. Thus, observing the mother of the puppies and finding out all you can about the father is absolutely essential.

Many years ago people acquired puppies from one of two categories. Either they wanted a magnificent show-quality specimen, in which case they expected to pay a premium price for the puppy, or, hoping for a lower price, they asked for the "runt" or one of the puppies that "wasn't good enough to show." In either case, breeders often gave them a puppy that wasn't going to go all the way to stardom and make the breeder famous. (He would have preferred to do that himself!) In the case of the lower priced puppy, the conscientious breeder often agreed to let the buyers have a lesser quality puppy but withheld the registration papers because he or she didn't want that puppy used for breeding later on.

Today, thanks to the educational efforts of breeders, veterinarians and university veterinary schools, most people realize that the expense and effort of caring for a good specimen is the same (and sometimes less!) than that of a poor one. Consequently, puppy buyers today look for a puppy that will grow up to be as representative of its breed as possible. And that's good for everyone concerned, even the puppies.

Breeders endeavor to apply their time, efforts and knowledge to breeding better dogs from the best parents they can use. Buyers are learning more about what goes into producing better dogs. And the dogs are being bred and raised to conform to the Standard of Perfection for their respective breeds, to be "typey" and—above all—to live useful, fulfilling, healthy lives.

The word *conformation* is defined by the dictionary as meaning structure. Since we cannot talk about the structure of puppies without recognizing that, in most cases, they inherit their structure from their parents, we must look first at the parents. Occasionally a puppy will develop poor conformation due to an abnormality, sickness or accident.

This leads us to a discussion of *type*. Type in dogs refers to a certain image of common characteristics. Type is so important that dog show judges are constantly looking for it in the dogs they evaluate in the breed ring because they know that the correct type dogs are going to be the breeding stock of the future.

One of the best examples of what we mean by type can be found in the hunting breeds. If you go to a breed show and look at the conformation of English Setters, for example, you would find a very specific "type" of English Setter. He would probably be large boned, tall with a magnificent head, low-set ears and a lot of long hair (called *feathering*) under his chest and behind his four legs. In addition, he would carry a tail with equally long hair underneath it which swayed when he moved. The whole image of the dog would be grace and fluidity when he was gaited or moved around the ring.

To see a different "type" of English Setter you have only to go to a field trial. There the English Setters would be smaller in size, finer boned with shorter, narrower muzzles and almost no long feathering at all. The reason for the enormous difference in the "types" of English Setters is easy to understand once we think about it. Those dogs shown in the breed ring are referred to as "bench" dogs and those used in hunting are called "field" dogs.

In the breed ring, dog fanciers are looking for the beauty and conformation of the dog. Because bench setters are heavier boned and larger, they would not move as effortlessly and for as long a period of time as their lighter weight cousins. Furthermore, the magnificent feathering of bench dogs would soon be torn away by the brush and tussocks through which they run. In other words, bench dogs are bred specifically as companions to man with some of the natural instincts of the breed lessened by selective breeding practices.

Field dogs, on the other hand, are bred to work. From the genetic foundation of the puppies to the final months of training for the mature adult, these dogs have one thing on their mind—work in the field. And if they were entered into competition in the breed ring, most would look like poor relatives to the statuesque larger dogs. Type, then, is a matter of choice in this case. The informed potential dog owner would decide which type of English Setter best suited his or her needs before making the final decision.

Sometimes type is a lot less obvious to the inexperienced eye, and a lot less significant in one's final choice of a bloodline. Take, for example, Miniature Schnauzers. There are several types, all of which are correct and all of which are appealing to the Miniature Schnauzer fancier. It's simply a matter of which "type" a person prefers. More times than not, people who obtain a Miniature Schnauzer puppy have no idea of type and don't learn about it until their puppy is mature. And I know of many people who have lived with Miniature Schnauzers for years and not only aren't aware of type, but could care even less.

In this case, there are many subtle differences, such as length of muzzle and shape of head. The Standard of Perfection for the breed states that Miniature Schnauzers shall be square dogs with level toplines. "Square" means that they should be as tall at the withers, or shoulders, as they are long from the chest to the end of the body. Level topline simply means that they should measure the same height at the top of the shoulders (withers) as they do at the top of the hip (croup). In other words, when you look at them in a profile view, you should not see a slope from the shoulders down to the tail.

The slight difference in Miniature Schnauzer type can come in what appears to be the length of back, for instance. To the untrained eye two dogs can appear to have differing back lengths yet when measured they are the same. However, the neck, head and legs can make one dog appear to have a longer back than the other, and the experienced fancier can spot the difference and may have certain preferences regarding which type he likes best.

Since we are attempting to learn what goes into puppies to make them the dogs they will be, we must become aware of type and learn what it means. Only then can we decide if, in fact, type will be an important consideration in the final development of a puppy. Can you imagine, for example, the disappointment of a person who sees a regal looking English Setter breed champion, buys a puppy from a field line and then wonders for the rest of the dog's life why it never grew up to look like the dog originally seen?

One of the surest ways to find out what a puppy will look like when it becomes an adult is to look at puppies from earlier litters by the same parents. Also, the track record of what the sire produces, bred either to the bitch in question or similar type bitches, can be a good indicator for future puppies. If you look at several of the dam's progeny you will be able to get a picture of the average type of dog she produces. In doing so, you can estimate what a puppy from her present litter, bred by the same or similar type sire, will probably grow up to look like. In other words, study the earlier offspring of the puppies' parents for signs of what they will produce in the future.

Find out if some of the puppies from earlier litters are being shown in the breed ring for conformation, in obedience trials or in field work. If they are, go to see them and evaluate how they perform when compared with competitors. A proven record of performance in any endeavor says a lot for the dog and its breeding. And you can be sure that an impressive list of accomplishments is a pretty accurate forecaster for the future.

In looking at the breed traits of the puppies' parents, one should first be familiar with breed purpose. For example, hounds should have good scenting ability and the will to follow a trail. Bird dogs should be "birdie" and have soft mouths with which to carry game, unmarked, back to the hunter. Guard dogs should be alert, willing to please and courageous. Herding dogs should react well to eye contact, have excellent peripheral vision and be quick to respond to their master's commands.

Whether or not a puppy buyer intends to put the dog to work is really not the point. The fact remains that if a person chooses a Cocker Spaniel, for example, he should do so for more than the reason of long ears and a docked tail. It's all well and good to admire certain cosmetic features of a particular breed, but the buyer must consider that he will live with the dog for many years, and the intangible traits of his chosen breed should be equally important to him. After all, those intangible traits probably did a lot to convince the buyer to choose that breed in the first place. Therefore, consideration of the breed traits of the parents and how strongly they appear in the adults will give some clue of how strongly they will manifest themselves in the puppies.

The old saying, "What you see is what you get," seems fairly apropos to dog breeding. For example, if the buyer wishes to purchase a dog for the purpose of exhibiting and competing in obedience trials, it would be foolish to buy a breed that for centuries has been bred to work independently of man and has little or no instinctual traits of trainability. The best way I know of learning about breed traits and how they affect the man-dog relationship is to read. In other words, do your homework before you make up your mind about which breed you should be considering.

It's important to know, for example, that all breeds of dogs are predisposed to certain breed traits that you may or may not find suitable. The tendency to bite is one. Generally, breeds that carry strong fighting ability traits are more likely to bite than those that do not. Some breeds are easily stimulated to bark, others need a lot of excitement before they vocalize. And lead training a puppy is more difficult in aggressive breeds than in nonaggressive ones.

Most libraries stock numerous books on breeds of dogs, their histories and purposes. The American Kennel Club (AKC) publishes

What these young Irish Wolfhounds grow up to be will depend in part on their inheritance, which is already fixed, and their environment which waits ahead. A favorable blend of both will result in a beautiful dog that is also a pleasure to own.　　　　　　—Fess

Bloodhound puppies: a natural aptitude for trailing and a legendary sense of smell are standard features with this old breed.　　　　　　—Evelyn M. Shafer

a fine volume listing all the breeds acceptable for registration with them. In *The Complete Dog Book* they also give thorough coverage of breeds that are little known because they aren't among the most popular breeds, yet are registerable with the AKC.

If you're wondering what criteria you should use to choose the right breed, see Chapter 8. In it we go into the details of you and your unique circumstances and needs. Also, in the back of this book there is a list of all the AKC registerable breeds of dogs with some additional comments about their traits.

Environment

Now here's a subject that can really tell the tale of a puppy's future! As a puppy buyer, it is to your best interest to observe the environment of the parents as carefully as possible. Of course, you may never get the opportunity to see where and how the sire lives, but you can ask questions, listen and weigh the answers and comments that follow. And then there's always the "track record" of the sire.

Find out if the sire is a breed champion (his pedigree should tell you that). If he's a sporting dog, does he work in the field with the hunter? A hound may be raced in lure coursing and if he is, you should find out about it. How does he stand up to competition? If the sire is a working breed, has his trainability and willingness to please been tested in the obedience ring? If you are considering a toy or nonsporting breed, find out what kind of a companion to his master he really is. On a scale of 1 to 10, how does he rate?

In short, find out as much as you can about what kind of home the sire comes from and what he does with his owners besides eat and sleep. A dog that functions and participates in the lives of his owners is surely more able to cope with his world than one that does nothing but decorate a sofa. If the dog participates in activities, regardless of what those activities might be, he will likely transfer his ability to his progeny.

The environment of the dam is even more important than that of the sire for several reasons, not the least of which is physical condition (about which we will go into detail in Chapter 2). For now, let's look at where and how the dam lives. Some questions here should be: Does she live in the house, in a kennel, in a fenced yard or does she run free through the streets? Obviously, the more control there is over her home environment, the better she will be able to raise a litter of healthy, happy puppies.

Although a kennel can be spotlessly clean and spaciously built, there is no doubt in my mind that a kennel atmosphere creates more stress than that of a private home simply because there are more dogs in general in a kennel than in most homes. If, however, the kennel has a "whelping room" the atmosphere can be improved markedly to create a quieter, more peaceful atmosphere in which the dam can spend the final days of her pregnancy and the weeks during which she raises the puppies. Providing there is plenty of contact with humans and the bitch is comfortable, a "whelping room" environment would be perfectly acceptable.

Being locked in a fenced yard with little interaction with humans may provide lots of fresh air and sunshine for the dam, but it would hardly be considered an ideal environment in which to raise a potential brood bitch. Of course, any dog given the "freedom" of the streets will be lucky to reach breeding age let alone actually live long enough to successfully raise a litter of healthy puppies.

As I mentioned, the home seems to be the best place to house a bitch intended for breeding. The experiences she has in actually living with people cannot be duplicated or found anywhere else. The phone rings, the vacuum cleaner hums, the doorbell announces the arrivals of visitors, children run and play and life is busy. In a home environment the dam learns to cope with living and becomes adjusted to the realities of life both for herself and her family. Her pulse rate remains stable, her adrenalin works more efficiently and she learns to use all her senses to their fullest without overworking any of them.

Finally, when the home-raised dog is put to work either hunting in the field, exhibiting in obedience, racing, pulling sleds, whatever the activity, she becomes a well-rounded dog. In short, she lives, works and plays with humans—that's the kind of bitch that will make a good mother to her offspring.

Of course, I realize that there are many superior brood bitches who never get to see the outside of a kennel and whelping room, yet produce top-quality puppies. Mostly the reason for this is that the breeder simply cannot bring all of his or her dogs into the human living quarters, so he or she has to provide the next best kind of environment possible. Providing the bitch has the potential to learn to cope, that she is sound of mind and body to begin with because of her own sound breeding in the first place, and also providing she is bred to an equally sound sire, then the puppies will have the same potential. What the breeder and the puppy buyer do with that potential in the puppies is what the remainder of this book is all about.

Basically, what we're saying here is that if the owners of the sire and dam really care about their dogs and if they make every effort to practice good management and encourage the animals to fulfill a useful purpose within the human community by providing them with as many experiences in living as possible, then the dogs' potential to be good parents will be optimized. In short, in your search for just the right puppy, never overlook the environment of its parents.

Mixed Breeds

More than 40 years ago a scientist by the name of C. R. Stockard did some experimental studies on the modifications of forms in some pure breeds of dogs and their hybrid progeny. Allowing for time in which the progeny grew to maturity and themselves reproduced, he then published some interesting papers at the Wistar Institute in Philadelphia, Pennsylvania. For his work, Stockard chose Basset Hounds and German Shepherd Dogs because they varied greatly in size and conformation.

The original breeding pair and their offspring plus the second generation of offspring are pictured in a book titled *Genetics For Dog Breeders* by Dr. Frederick B. Hutt (W. H. Freeman & Co.). Photos of the first generation dogs showed medium-sized bodies and shorter legs than their German Shepherd Dog sire but longer legs than their Basset Hound dam.

By the next generation (F2), Stockard bred some short-legged dogs, some medium-legged dogs, and some with the long legs of the sire. In addition, their body shapes varied greatly as did the shape and expression of the heads. Actually, a few of the second generation dogs were rather good looking, but the majority were rather odd in appearance. Therein lies one of the major problems with mixed breeds—unpredictable form. The other big problem is the unpredictability of temperament.

Most people like to know what they're getting for their money before they buy. Whether you acquire ("The dear little thing that was left on my doorstep") or buy a mixed breed dog, there is absolutely no way anyone can predict what that cute little puppy is going to look or act like when he grows up. I have known many people who adopted adorable little furry puppies only to have them grow into long-legged monsters who needed a 1,000-acre ranch to roam on! I've also seen some nice little puppies turn out to be very nice little dogs. Again, nobody with an ounce of sense can guarantee the outcome of a mixed breed dog simply because nobody can document his pedigree.

Veterinarians and dog people are frequently asked to "guesti-mate" the outcome of a mixed breed puppy. In some, certain breed traits are quite obvious. In others, it's anybody's guess. But whatever the guess, I have never met a person who would guarantee the final results of the mating of two different breeds of dogs, whether they be two different pure breeds or one pure breed and one mixed breed or two mixed breeds. It's just not possible to know what the puppy will grow up to look or act like.

Once a mixed breed puppy is born, however, the way it is raised will have a lasting effect on its behavior as an adult. But one can be sure that no amount of early socialization and/or training can remove the predisposition to certain genetic traits that were set the moment that puppy was conceived. Often, early work with the puppy will mold it into a very delightful adult. Sometimes, no amount of effort on the part of the humans in its life can alter certain undesirable genetic traits.

I have worked with behavior problems in dogs for many years and have seen more mixed breeds than pure breds come to my office. Frequently, the owners had sought help from a variety of other people before coming to me. In the majority of cases, altering the human response to the dog's behavior resulted in satisfactory improvement. However, of all the cases I've seen that did not result in some form of behavioral modification, mixed breed dogs were the leaders. Some of them were so hyperactive, so wild, so shy, so aggressive or so untrained that only a course of heavy medication prescribed by a veterinarian over an extended period of time (or a lifetime!) could have helped. Even then, there was always the possibility that the medical treatment wouldn't work or new problems would arise or the old ones would reemerge at some future time. In every case, it meant heartbreak to those who loved the dogs and brought them to me for help. Whether or not the owners chose to attempt rehabilitation of the dogs or to get rid of their problems, usually through euthanasia, the outcome was grim.

On the plus side, however, there seems to be a certain vigor and vitality about some mixed breeds that enable them to survive certain illnesses and other adversities, such as parasites, better than their purebred cousins. Little research has been done on this by scientists, as few breeders would spend the time, money and effort to attempt such a study. However, mongrels in many species of animals have been found to be better able to cope and survive. Mongrel chickens, for instance, frequently produce more eggs than purebreds. Certain cross-bred beef cattle reach market weight much sooner than purebreds. But the deliberate breeding of mongrel dogs, for the purpose of bettering the species, seems a long way off.

The best test of continuity in any breed is its predictability. The successful breeding of purebred dogs has been going on for centuries, and it took many generations to develop the breeds we know today.

We have paintings, prose and poetry by some of the world's earliest artists and writers that tell of these breeds. Whether it be by pen or paint, these descriptions recorded clear images of the form, temperament and purpose of each breed of purebred dogs. No one then and no one now can accurately predict the ultimate outcome of mixed breed dogs. There's an old adage that says, "Let the buyer beware." I sometimes think it was written by someone who bought a mixed breed dog that didn't work out.

Puppy Sources

Puppies can be bought from pet shops, breeders, dealers and even some animal shelters who sell puppies at nominal fees just to get them into good homes. Some shelters place their grown dogs and puppies free of charge. All shelters want their dogs to have the best opportunity to fit into the family's lifestyle.

Whether the shelters place purebred dogs or mixed breeds, they try to make certain the placement will be right for all concerned before they release the dog. They often follow up with phone calls and visits to the adoption home to be sure everything is going well.

One must realize, however, that adopting a dog or puppy limits the available information regarding the dog's heritage. This factor would be crucial to someone planning to show the dog in breed competition, but not at all important to a person who was looking for a good pet for the family.

Pet shops and dealers are not necessarily the breeders of the puppies they sell. Consequently, they too would not have full knowledge of the puppy's background. Only a breeder would know all about the background of the parents. Therefore, though puppies can be acquired from a variety of sources, a person's own circumstances and requirements frequently determine the source of his or her puppy.

Conclusion

When we begin to examine what turns a puppy into the dog it will become, we must first look at its parents and earlier ancestors. Its genetic history will tell us a lot about what's behind the little fellow, and from that, we can begin to draw a picture of what it will look and act like.

Scientists and geneticists have proven that a puppy's conformation, emotional and mental stability, and even intelligence are, to some degree, predisposed by heredity. In short, the genes of the puppy have set the stage for the production that follows. Whether or not that production becomes a stellar performance or a miserable failure depends on many things, not the least of which is what happens to the zygote once it is formed.

Such factors as the temperament, physical and mental health, conformation threshold of adaptability, behavioral traits, performance records and environment of the puppy's parents all contribute to the creation of a healthy fetus. Finally, man must then mold that set of genes into a pleasant, responsive dog he can call a "companion."

2

In Utero Environment

NOW THAT WE'VE established the importance of genetics in general and the genetic background of the parents of a puppy in particular, we move on to consider the dam, the mating and the whelping of the litter. As mentioned in the first chapter, raising a puppy is a lot like building a house. We'll consider the genetic background of the parents, or the litter's gene bank, as the building blocks we're going to use.

Let's compare the dam and her management to the operation of a sophisticated manufacturing plant. After all, she really is a sophisticated machine capable of producing some highly complex products. For the sake of our example, let's assume this manufacturing plant is going to produce all the supplies we'll use to construct our house.

First, we need to ascertain that the factory is capable of taking the raw product and, using that sophisticated machinery, turning out quality building materials. In other words, the dam should be a quality dog—emotionally, physically and mentally—whose body and organs function as they were intended. Just as a quality factory is designed to produce quality products, we must keep in mind that a quality brood bitch is capable of producing quality puppies.

This imaginary factory of ours runs along smoothly for most of the year requiring regular maintenance, but no particular "high-stress" care. Suddenly, a huge order arrives and the machines are shifted into high gear. Because the machinery has been properly maintained on a regular basis, it shifts into "high-stress" production smoothly and without incident. As the motors whirl and the wheels and gears turn, the machines reach peak performance without hesitation.

That's exactly what happens to the brood bitch. Most of the year, her body functions normally and without incident. She eats, sleeps, exercises, goes through heat cycles and comes out again due, of course, to proper management by her owners. Then comes the time for her to be bred. The machinery of her body goes into "high-stress" status and begins to prepare her for peak production.

Once the bitch has been bred, she remains in the "high-stress" category for approximately sixty-three days as the sophisticated machinery of her reproductive organs manufactures the product, puppies. Finally, our factory delivers the finished products. No longer needing to maintain top production status, the machine's control panels gradually switch to care-giving running speed. There it will stay until the factory gets another "high-stress" call or returns to normal maintenance.

As the bitch prepares to whelp her litter, her body automatically gears itself for the delivery. Heart rate rises slightly, breathing rate increases and a whole series of muscular contractions begin, all specifically designed to help the puppies make the trip through the birth canal.

Once the puppies are born, the bitch's body begins to function as a care-giving machine. It provides nourishment, warmth and the means to keep the puppies clean and healthy until such time as they can care for themselves. When they can survive and function on their own, her body functions gradually return to normal operating speed once more. The manufacturing plant has realized its purpose and produced a quality product when called upon to do so and, like the factory, the bitch's job was completed when she whelped and raised a quality litter.

All the materials needed to build a quality house have now been produced. How we build the house will be up to us. So it is with the bitch. With the help of proper management, she has produced quality puppies. How we raise those puppies will be up to us, but one thing is sure. The end result of the human effort from this point on will have a profound effect on the results. We will delve deeply into that effort in future chapters, but right now we are concerned with the specifics of production. Let's examine, in detail, the important elements that go into the production of a healthy litter. With that in mind, we must begin with the dam herself.

Age of Dam

Brood bitches are capable of whelping litters from their first estrus to well up into mid-life, anywhere from eight to 11 years of age. But that doesn't really say what most people want to know about age and breeding. All it does say is that veterinary medical practitioners are giving us a general guide to the age limits for conception.

A bitch that is being bred for the first time, sometimes referred to as a "maiden bitch," should be bred after she matures and before age four or five. In many breeds, particularly the smaller breeds, bitches mature by one year of age. In the larger breeds, it may take two, even three years for a bitch to mature. In most breeds, however, bitches are mature by the time they are 18 to 24 months of age.

Breeding a bitch before she reaches maturity can create many problems. It's like a twelve-year-old girl having a baby: she's just not ready to be a mother. Frequently, both the mother and babies suffer.

The body of an immature bitch is still busy developing. It has not yet developed the capacity to cope with reproduction and all its ramifications. One good example of this is the mature bitch's ability to produce a hormone known as prolactin. Prolactin stimulates the flow of milk and care-giving behavior. If an immature bitch cannot produce her own prolactin, she can hardly be expected to give proper care and nourishment to her puppies.

Also, by forcing a young, immature body to reproduce itself, the body may be stressed beyond its limits and self-development ceases so that the mother never will realize her fullest potential. Further, an overstressed body cannot offer optimum care to the unborn fetuses and, later, to the newborn litter for the puppies' development.

Finally, an immature bitch is usually not emotionally ready to handle motherhood, so again the puppies suffer. If she's not ready to whelp it is common for her to neglect the puppies once they are born. (I have personally known several immature bitches that killed their entire litters shortly after whelping in what appeared to be states of hysteria and frenzy! It appeared, at the time, that they had no idea of what was happening to them and instinctively tried to destroy some sort of vermin that suddenly appeared in their beds.)

On the other end of the age scale, an older bitch that is being bred for the first time should pass a careful veterinary examination before she is mated. Once cleared for breeding, the veterinarian should supervise not only her gestation period, but be handy at whelping time. Older bitches may experience difficulty in delivering their first litter if they are beyond the age of four years.

Scientists feel that litter size is about 10 percent hereditary, and the other 90 percent is due to a multiplicity of factors. Certainly the age of the dam is one factor. Most breeders find that a mature bitch will have large litters, whereas immature and bitches eight years and over generally produce smaller litters. Fertility seems to rise and fall in direct relationship to age.

Once a bitch has produced a litter of puppies, and providing she is maintained in top condition, she can produce many more litters in her lifetime.

Physical Condition of Dam

Before she's bred, the dam should be in excellent physical condition, well muscled and in proper weight for her breed and particular structure. A small, fine-boned bitch will naturally weigh less than her heavy-boned sister. She should be neither too lean nor too fat. She should have a healthy looking, clean coat and clear eyes, nose and ears. In other words, she should look like she's in good physical condition. But that's not all.

She should act like she's feeling fine. Sometimes a dog will appear to be in good health, yet actually be suffering from some physical problem that she has only recently acquired and that has not yet shown up in her overall appearance. In Chapter 1, we discussed abnormalities and physical problems that are either dangerous to the bitch or that may have an adverse effect on any puppies she might have. Some of these abnormalities can even prove lethal to her puppies.

It is important to remember that, if a bitch is going to be bred, she will need to have as much going for her as possible. She will be in whelp for approximately 63 days, and following delivery she'll nourish and care for them for anywhere from three to eight more weeks. All the while, her body will be strained to its limit. It will be too late, once she's bred or once the puppies are born, to put her in good condition. So, if we want to raise the best possible dogs, we'd better make certain that their mother is in the best possible condition to bring them into this world and get them started toward adulthood.

An ideal brood bitch is one that is slightly oversize or has a slight overlength to her body. Many breeders have found that this type of bitch carries her puppies well and has less trouble at whelping time than a smaller sized bitch or one with a shortened body length. It should be understood that when we speak of the conformation of the brood bitch, we are looking for one that has good overall looks and is representative of her breed.

Parasites are a real problem to a bitch in whelp. Therefore, she should be free of both internal and external parasites before breeding time. Parasites drain the bitch of vital energy and blood and can threaten the life of the fetuses. In addition, some parasites, such as fleas, give the bitch other problems, such as tapeworms.

The brood bitch should receive all immunizations before breeding. By immunizing her against distemper, hepatitis, leptospirosis, parainfluenza, parvovirus and rabies about six to eight weeks before you expect her to come into season, she will have built up a sufficient amount of antibodies to pass on to her puppies via the colostrum, or first milk. By neglecting this important phase of good management, you will be placing the puppies at a disadvantage when they are weaned. Leaving puppies unprotected against these diseases could cost you the litter.

Bitches with irregular or abnormal heat cycles are not good candidates for breeding. Abnormal seasons may indicate a problem with the bitch's physiology, which could jeopardize the bitch's safety or create undesirable hereditary factors in the puppies. A well-known veterinarian once told me that he felt bitches with false pregnancies were nature's way of preventing a particular bitch from ever whelping a litter. Furthermore, he said, when those bitches were bred through veterinary intervention, they failed to produce normal puppies or lost the puppies during or shortly after whelping.

Finally, if a brood bitch has ever had a broken limb, spinal or skin problems, major surgery, a serious viral illness or any problem that may have damaged the liver, her breeding should be supervised by a veterinarian.

Management of the Mating

It is not the intention here to discuss the hows and wherefores of mating (see the back of this book for a listing of books on mating

Sealyham Terriers: A family portrait. With many white breeds full pigmentation is not achieved, in some cases, until several weeks after birth.

An even, attractive litter of black Pugs.

dogs). Rather, we will limit our discussion to some relative points on the management of a mating as it relates to the many factors that go into making a puppy the dog it will become. In that context, there are several things we should think about.

First, when planning a mating it is wise to arrange breeding dates, if there are to be several, within 48 hours of each other. Bitches that are bred several times over a period longer than 48 hours tend to experience complications at whelping time. This could be because there are several periods of conception involved and the fetuses are in several stages of readiness for whelping when the first fetus begins presentation. The muscular contractions involved for the presentation of the first fetus also react on any later-conceived fetuses in the uterus. If the later-conceived fetuses are not ready for delivery, the bitch can have problems in delivery, and those puppies will not reach optimum growth within the uterus.

The place of mating should offer peace and quiet to both the bitch and the stud. When there is unnecessary noise and confusion, either or both dogs can become so stressed and worried that a mating does not take place at all. In that case, frustration for all concerned can be the end result.

Occasionally, a dominant bitch will not allow a subordinate male to breed. Conversely, a dominant male may not be able to breed an extremely subordinate bitch simply because, every time he approaches her, she rolls over on her back. Ideally, the bitch should be slightly subordinate to the male. In that case, the male will assume the leadership role in the breeding process and the ovulating bitch will cooperate by allowing the male to mount and enter her.

Bitches that are overhumanized by their owners are usually difficult to breed and frequently experience serious problems at whelping time and later. If the bond between the dog and owner is too strong, as seen in some bitches who have been trained for specific behaviors to such an excess that they are constantly worried about the whereabouts of their owners, then the raising of a litter of puppies can be overly stressful to the dam. I know of two bitches, both with extremely strong bonds to their owners through obedience training and competition, who made terrible mothers although they experienced no problems whelping. They were simply so torn between their devotion to their owners and their jobs as mothers that they became sick and were unable to properly raise their offspring. Unfortunately, the puppies suffered because they did not get optimum care and attention from their mothers at a time when it was so critical.

41

Admittedly, two cases don't necessarily make a good argument, but many breeders have told me similar stories. Further, most breeders claim their best brood bitches are those that are loved, cared for, occasionally shown in the breed rings, but used primarily as brood bitches, nothing else. What these people seem to be saying is that being a good brood bitch is a job in itself and the successful breeder recognizes this and manages brood bitches to be good producers.

The final point to be considered in the management of a good mating has to do with the people involved. Many dogs, both studs and bitches, have very definite idiosyncrasies when it comes to the actual courting and copulation process. They can be so distracted by the presence of strangers that they do not relax and concentrate on the job at hand. Instead, they spend the entire time worrying about the strangers in their midst rather than breeding. The stress created by this type of a situation hardly seems to constitute an ideal breeding atmosphere.

Management of the Dam

As we've pointed out several times, we must think of the dam as a highly sophisticated machine. If this machine is going to produce a quality product, then the general management of her living conditions becomes critically important. First, we must consider nutrition.

The bitch should be fed a well-balanced diet at all times. When breeding time arrives, she should be offered even more nutritionally high-powered food. Many commercial dog food companies manufacture food specifically designed to meet the requirements of bitches in whelp, lactating bitches and young puppies. Each one is clearly marked to define its purpose and contents, and most veterinarians are prepared to advise the bitch's owner on a quality diet for the mother-to-be. The need for vitamins and mineral supplements will be determined by the quality of the food she is eating before, during and after preganancy. Here again, a competent veterinary practitioner should help the bitch's owner decide what and how the diet should be supplemented.

The consequence of a good or poor quality diet is what we are concerned with here. Puppies born to a bitch who has received a proper diet while in whelp will obviously have many health advantages over puppies whose dam struggled for her own survival during that time. Therefore, knowing what kind of condition the dam was maintained in during pregnancy becomes of great importance.

For the dog fancier who is breeding a litter of puppies for the first time, those same books on breeding mentioned earlier have excellent sections on diet and care included in them. It is not the intent here to expound on the nutritional requirements of breeding stock, but merely to point out that it is an important factor.

Most dams will have varying nutritional demands at various stages of pregnancy and during the nursing stage. For example, a few weeks before she whelps, the dam may indicate a need for more food. At this time a small addition (about ¼ the normal amount) may satisfy her. Once she begins nursing a litter, particularly a large one, her daily consumption may increase by three times its normal volume.

Of course, when the dam consumes more food, she will feel the need to evacuate more frequently. Consequently, it must be kept in mind that she will need more opportunities to get outdoors and relieve herself. In addition, as the puppies grow within the horns of the uterus, pressure will be applied to the bladder and she will need to urinate more frequently.

One final note: Any medication given to the dam while she is in whelp or while she is nursing should only be prescribed by a veterinarian. To administer any kind of drugs otherwise is to possibly endanger the dam or the litter.

Feeding for Optimum Breeding

Dr. Donald Collins offers the following nutrition guide for the brood bitch.

The proper feeding of the dam begins, not when one discovers she is pregnant, but, indeed, when she herself is a puppy. Only by properly nourishing the immature bitch can one assure themselves that she will have a reproductive tract that is healthy and normal in size, and ovaries that maximize egg output when the bitch reaches sexual maturity.

Potential brood bitches should be given special dietary attention from the moment they, themselves, are whelped. While she is a rapidly growing puppy, the potential dam should be fed a diet containing high levels of usable protein and energy. The amount she is fed should be sufficient to bring her to her optimum size and weight, but never in an attempt to push her to her maximum weight potential. Once she has reached sexual maturity, she should be kept in an optimal nutritional state by feeding her a diet that is known to adequately support maintenance.

Not all bitches have enjoyed the feeding program just described. Every new breeding bitch should be made ready by reviewing her diet for any nutritional deficiencies, and by correcting any that are present before she comes into heat. Bitches that are too fat may not ovulate or, if they do, will produce very few ova. Generally pups whelped by fat bitches are few in number, but large in size—so large in fact that they may lead to a difficulty at birth. Overweight bitches should have their food restricted in order to reduce their weight to optimum before they come into heat. Underweight bitches should be fed a diet suitable for a lactating bitch. If either over- or underweight bitches have not reached their optimum weight and condition by the time their breeding date arrives, they should not be bred until their next heat.

The nourishment of the bitch for the three to four months prior to her pregnancy is almost as important as the nourishment while she is in whelp, since some of the nutrients she puts into her puppies come from her nutrient stores, not from the food she is fed during pregnancy. If her feeding plan has not adequately supplied nutrients and energy, the bitch in whelp will obtain them by robbing her own body tissues. If neither dietary nor body sources of nutrients and energy are available, a multitude of problems can result.

Once bred, the bitch should be fed a high-quality maintenance diet. During the last three weeks of pregnancy, the bitch's food intake may be increased by about 25 percent of her usual consumption. Don't feed her any more than this.

When dietary failures occur during pregnancy, they usually can be traced back to the feeding of either an imbalanced diet or a diet containing insufficient nutrients and energy to support the pregnancy. Those failures most likely to be recognized are:

1. An "out of condition" appearance of the bitch. This may not become apparent until after the pups are born. An actual loss in body weight throughout gestation can occur, but is unusual in most instances.
2. An uncontrollable diarrhea in the bitch following whelping and throughout much of lactation. This is most often seen when the bitch must increase her food intake excessively to

The condition of this Cocker Spaniel dam is a credit to the person looking after her and her puppies.

Healthy neonatal puppies, like these Canaan Dogs, show an unmistakable series of behaviors. The observant breeder always watches for signs of health or illness in the nest.

meet increased lactational demands because the food she is eating is poorly digestible or low in calories.

3. The "fading puppy" syndrome. The puppy may appear normal at birth, but several hours to several days later it is found crying or whimpering and chilled. It is off by itself, obviously disowned by the bitch. Attempts to reunite the two are usually met with failure. The puppy's stomach will be empty and its body will be dehydrated. When weighed, it will weigh the same or less than the day before.

4. Anemias. When an anemia occurs as the result of a dietary deficiency during reproduction, it will be present in both the dam and pup. When both mother and pup are anemic, the first place to look for its cause is the diet.

No supplements should be added at any time during gestation. For some dog feeders, supplementation has become such a way of life that they place more emphasis on the supplement they use than on the food they feed. As with any other phase of a dog's life cycle, the ill-advised use of food supplements during pregnancy can cause great harm.

Exercise

A regular schedule of exercise is essential to the health of the pregnant bitch. In the early stages of pregnancy, her normal routine is desirable, providing she gets a good amount of exercise. However, as the weeks pass and the bitch begins to get heavy, her exercise program should be cut back in the amount of time, energy and distance. Note that it is advised to *cut back* not *cut out*. She should be allowed to set her own pace of walking, running, playing or whatever form her exercise takes. When she begins to appear winded and tired allow her to stop. She should never be forced to do more than she can reasonably do without showing signs of fatigue.

A regular exercise routine will help her develop proper muscle tone, which will help the bitch, owner and puppies during delivery. Puppies that are slowly expelled can suffer irreparable brain damage or die due to lack of oxygen. Here again, the breeder can aid the bitch in producing a healthy litter or a sickly one simply by proper management and help if the need arises. Certainly, she should not be treated roughly or abused at any time, pregnant or not.

Housing

The special housing requirements of a pregnant bitch and a bitch raising a litter of puppies are much different from the dam's normal living quarters. During the early stages of pregnancy, no special housing facilities are necessary providing she has protection from wind, rain, cold and heat. Actually, most bitches seem to prefer their regular sleeping and living quarters at this time, probably because they don't feel any different than they do when they're not pregnant.

Several weeks before the bitch is due to whelp, however, she should be introduced to the quarters she will use for delivery and raising the puppies. Again, there is a great deal of literature available on whelping boxes, special crates and unique types of delivery areas that breeders can make themselves or purchase. Therefore, we will discuss here only those aspects that affect the puppies and their delivery, health, safety and development.

In the case of the individual dog owner with a bitch about to whelp, the selection of a maternity area depends on the domestic situation within the home. If the bitch is normally a house dog, then she would probably do well in the kitchen or laundry room area. Of course we are assuming that, if there are children in the home, they are well-mannered, reasonably quiet, and over the age of toddlers. In this situation, the bitch will have opportunities to see and hear her family, yet still be able to retreat to her maternity corner to rest and care for her young. The family with very young children should find a place where the bitch can feel a part of the home life, yet not be in the midst of noisy, active babies and toddlers. Human babies do not understand the needs of baby puppies and can, if not supervised carefully, seriously injure the puppies.

Bitches that live primarily in a yard or outdoor kennel do not have to be brought into the house to be comfortable when whelping. They should have a maternity area designed for them that closely resembles their normal living quarters yet provides the extra measure of quiet and comfort they will need. Like all maternity areas, it should be warm, dry, draft-free and secure. Many dog owners choose to arrange a small area of a garage or workshop for this purpose. Ideally, it should be made so the bitch can come and go without allowing the puppies, as they learn to walk, to get outdoors without the owner's supervision.

Kennel owners usually provide a whelping room for brood bitches. This is an area or separate room isolated from the main part of the kennel, yet close enough to allow convenience of care and supervision by the owner. Most kennel brood bitches would be unhappy in a home environment unless they were previously accustomed to being in the house. Again, good management is the key to an optimum delivery and a happy bitch who is content with her job of raising her puppies.

Just as the bitch needed a quieter atmosphere in which to mate, she needs, now more than ever, a quiet place to whelp and raise her family. But, she also needs to feel a part of the home (or kennel) environment that she has always known and in which she feels secure. Therefore, the maternity area should be open to the family, within reason, and declared off-limits to visitors and strangers. A nervous, frightened bitch can either refuse to care for her puppies at all or be so upset that the puppies sense her anxiety and respond poorly to her efforts of care.

When deciding where to arrange the maternity area one should keep in mind ease of maintenance and availability of heat. The bitch will care for the puppies for the first two or three weeks, but after that it will become the owner's job. And the litter's nest, or bed, will need a great deal of attention from the day the bitch starts using it. Therefore, the nest should be a place where it can be kept spotlessly clean, dry and free of debris. Infections in puppies can be deadly.

Once the bitch starts to whelp, an auxilliary form of heat will probably be required for several days. Most breeders use an electric heating pad or an overhead bulb. Thus the availability of an electric outlet nearby should be ascertained before the final decision of a maternity area is made. Remember, cold puppies never do well and frequently don't survive.

Good management of the brood bitch begins by providing her with an optimum environment in which to deliver and raise her puppies. Anything less than optimum will adversely affect her emotional contentment. Remember, the maternity environment controls the delivery of the puppies and the bitch's happiness. Right from the first breath of life, a multitude of factors influences the outcome of a puppy.

Activities

Here we differentiate between activities and exercise, which has already been discussed. Activities are the things a bitch does in her normal routine of daily living—things such as going in the car with her owner, playing games of fetch, jumping, hiking, swimming, going to training classes, hunting in the field or just walking in the park.

The general rule of thumb says, let the bitch live her normal life for the first four weeks following the breeding. During the first month, the fetuses are developing heart, lungs, organs and brain. It isn't until the last half of the gestation period that they begin to develop bone. Therefore, the bitch may not even appear to be pregnant at first and will have her usual amount of energy and stamina. By continuing with her regular routine of activities she will maintain muscle tone, good health and a positive attitude toward life.

Beginning about the fifth week, the puppies will start to grow within her as they develop bone and flesh. Although many bitches show no signs of getting heavy until just before the whelping date, she may appear to grow in width, breathe more heavily as though she had just eaten a full meal and exhibit a tendency to limit her activities and rest more often. As the puppies become larger, they begin to press on her diaphragm, which presses on her lungs causing a shortness of breath.

Some mild form of physical activity should be offered to her every day—a short walk, a few tosses of a ball for her to retrieve, some special time set aside when she and the owner can quietly enjoy each other's company. If she shows signs of refusal, the activity should cease immediately; she knows better than any human what she feels comfortable doing and what stresses her.

Activities such as attending training classes, participating in field trials or any other competitive sports should be temporarily postponed. The fact that these activities involve other people and other dogs in places away from her home environment can jeopardize both the bitch and the puppies.

Unfortunately, many dogs carry diseases that the owners neglect to treat (or aren't even aware of!) and parasites can be passed quite easily to the bitch in whelp. Medicating for these problems, in most cases, cannot be undertaken so late in the bitch's pregnancy because her and/or her puppies' health would be endangered. Therefore, keeping her close to home during the latter part of her pregnancy is the best way to assure her health and safety. In addition, strenuous physical activities, even an accident or a dog fight, can so stress her that she may abort the puppies early. If this happens, the puppies will probably not be fully formed or will be born dead.

Emotional Factors

If a bitch in whelp lives with other dogs or pets, the owner should be aware that, as she slows down in her normal activities when the delivery date approaches, she should not be ignored in place of the more active pets. If she is, she will likely feel as though she were being punished or neglected by the otherwise attentive owner and become stressed. Further, she may look upon the other pets as threats to her security and become aggressive toward them.

The best way to handle interactions between the owner, the pregnant bitch and other pets is to let her set the pace. There will be times when she chooses to play and become involved with her human master and friends. And there will be times when she chooses to go off by herself for a period of quiet rest. As long as she isn't deliberately pushed out of the normal routine of activities, she will accept her temporary role gratefully and without feelings of animosity or neglect.

Finally, a bitch that normally lives in the house or yard with a private family should not be boarded in a kennel situation during pregnancy unless it is absolutely imperative that the family leave her there. As pointed out earlier, the environment with strange dogs jeopardizes both the mother and the puppies. In addition, she may be so upset at being left in a strange place that she will suffer physically. Vacations and times when a family must board the dog should be planned ahead so that the bitch in whelp will be in her home environment for the entire period of her pregnancy and until the puppies are weaned and gone.

Whelping Experience

Throughout this chapter, we've mentioned the bitch and how she copes with the actual whelping of her puppies in relationship to her environment. We've talked about physical health, comfort and safety. We've discussed how a conscientious breeder goes about ensuring the best possible litter from the best possible pair of dogs he or she can get their hands on.

In breeds the size of this Cocker Spaniel, a litter of seven is considered larger than average.
—*Evelyn M Shafer*

Boxer puppies will experience dynamic growth throughout their first year.
—*William Brown*

The final aspect we will cover here is the whelping experience itself. Once again, it is imperative to mention the importance of keeping strangers and visitors away from the dam and the maternity area until the puppies are several weeks old and getting around on their own. If they should become sick while the mother is still caring for them, they have less of a chance of surviving simply because they haven't built up enough immunities and strength to help them fight off the problem. Once they are mobile and beginning to eat solid food, however, it can be assumed that they have enough antibodies to resist most viruses or bacteria that may be introduced into their environment.

Furthermore, many bitches take the job of mothering very seriously. For the first week, sometimes more, a bitch will growl and may even bite anyone other than the owner who comes near her "den." It is the dam's maternal instinct that makes her hold the world at bay. This alone is reason enough to keep people away.

Occasionally a breeder will own the sire of the litter as well as the dam and this can cause some interesting ramifications. If the sire is allowed free access to the dam and the litter, the dam may even forbid the sire from going too close to the puppies for the first week or so. I have a friend who has just such a situation and it's always fascinating to watch the dogs interact with each other and the puppies. In this case, the dam allows the sire to come to the edge of the whelping box and peer in, but not touch. By week two, she allows him to help her clean the puppies and nuzzle them several times a day, but only when she's with them. If he should approach the litter box when she's away getting some exercise or a drink of water, she will come flying back snarling and growling at him. He, in turn, walks away as if to say, "Okay, I'll come back later." My friend never allows him to be present during whelping.

During the process of whelping, the owner is frequently the key to a successful whelping. The owner should not interfere with the whelping unless it is absolutely necessary. Instead, he or she should take up a support role and be there to reassure the dam, particularly a maiden dam, that all is well. The owner can assist the dam by removing a puppy from under the dam when she begins contractions for the next puppy. Keeping the whelping box clean and dry and supplying plenty of shredded newspaper helps the bitch concentrate on caring for the puppies rather than the nest itself. (You can purchase newspaper without the print from printers and newspaper publishers. The ink can be poisonous to puppies.)

As mentioned, any of the better books on whelping and raising puppies give detailed instructions on how to manage a delivery, so we will not go into details here. It should be pointed out, however, that the major responsibility of an owner at whelping time is to keep an eye out for trouble and seek help immediately. These books define the symptoms that could indicate a problem with delivery and should be studied well in advance of the delivery date.

A well-managed whelping experience will have direct results on the newborn puppies, and that is our role here. When a bitch delivers her litter in an atmosphere of emotional security and physical comfort, she will be better prepared to begin her mammoth job of raising her family to the best of her ability. When the dam puts all of herself into producing happy, healthy puppies, then the humans who will shortly come into the puppies' lives will have the raw material with which to mold and develop the best possible dog. (Remember the manufacturing plant that's geared for "high-stress" production?)

3

Birth Environment: Birth to 20 Days

THE FIRST 20 days of the puppies' lives form the period of the most rapid physical change they'll ever experience. In fact, the changes occur with such impetus that scientists have divided the period into two stages in an effort to more clearly define what and how things happen.

The *Neonatal Period* occurs from birth to 12 days of age. It is the beginning of the first critical period because survival is the main concern. The puppies are totally dependent on their mother for warmth, food, sleep and massage. At this stage puppies can suffer the most from physiological effects.

Although the puppies are living organisms, they have not fully developed in many areas. This lack of complete development makes them so vulnerable that failure of vital parts of the body can mean death. To make matters more complicated, the puppies do not have the strength and energy stored within their bodies to survive major problems simply because they haven't lived long enough.

From birth their appearance alters so drastically that you hardly recognize them from one day to the next. Newborn puppies are usually strange looking little creatures. They certainly don't look like the adults of their breed. They have short, stubby noses, eyelids that seem to be glued shut, little ear flaps plastered against the sides of their heads and short little legs that sprawl in every direction when they're lying down and dangle lifelessly when you pick them up.

At birth each puppy is only partially developed. It can neither see nor hear. Although heartbeat, balance mechanism and breathing are developed, its temperature regulation and metabolism are only partially developed.

It cannot walk because the muscles of the hindquarters are not yet developed. It crawls on its forelimbs by pulling itself along and it cannot back up at all. It uses its front paws to knead the mother's teats to stimulate the release of milk.

It has no teeth and cannot eliminate without stimulation from its mother or some soft, wet source such as a wet towel rubbed over its anogenital area.

The sensory nerves of touch and temperature are partially developed, making it possible for the puppy to distinguish between soft and hard surfaces and to locate its mother by the heat of her body. Thus the puppy only reacts to things that it can feel through direct touch to its body.

Although the puppy can feel pain at this point in its development, it responds poorly to it because its motor capacities are not fully developed. For example, if a puppy feels cold and discovers a warm resting place such as an electric heating pad, it will remain there despite the fact that the pad may become too hot and eventually kill the puppy.

The brain is not fully developed either, and the vocal chords are not mature, so it can only mew, squeek and whine. Its olfactory (smell) sense is not completely developed yet it can taste. And the development of its intellectual capacities aren't complete, so its investigative behaviors are limited to touch and temperature.

The sleep center in the brain is also not fully developed. Thus it spends most of its time sleeping. As the sleep center completes its development, activated sleep begins. This can be observed when the puppy twitches in its sleep, almost as if it were dreaming. The muscles of the limbs and hindquarters are strengthened through this activity so that, by the time the puppy is ready to walk, its motor muscles are strong enough to carry it.

In short, a newborn puppy is a pretty helpless little creature who has extremely simple needs and virtually no personality. It requires nutrition, sleep, warmth and massage—and time to grow.

The *Transition Period* occurs from 13 to 20 days of age and is the second part of the first critical period. It is so named because the

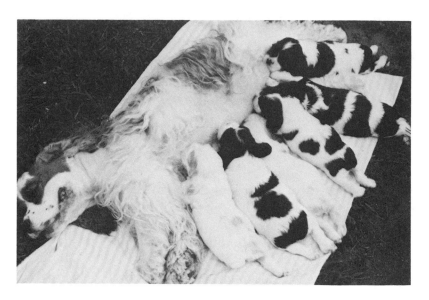

From birth . . .

To weaning . . .

To the big world of people and new experiences, this Cocker Spaniel litter is given every opportunity to develop into wonderful companions to their eventual owners.

—*Mary Jones*

puppies make the transition from helplessness to the stage when they begin to take notice of their environment and function on their own. The Transition Period begins with the opening of the eyes at approximately 13 days and ends when the startle response activates at 20 days of age.

In this chapter we will discuss, in detail, how the puppies change as they begin to complete development of their mental, physical and emotional abilities. In addition we'll discuss both the Neonatal Period and the Transition Period under each of these aspects. In this way, we'll follow the early development of the puppies to see how their birth environment affects them for the rest of their lives. It is important to remember, however, that the critical stages are average time slots, and one must allow for a range of variation in breeds of dogs as well as within each litter.

Environmental Temperature

Once the puppies are born, we must accept their genetic background and concentrate on the effect their environment will have on them as they develop. Their environment consists of their dam, their littermates, the people and other animals with which they come in contact and the place they live in. Thus it is easy to see why their environment will play a primary role in making them the dogs they will become.

It is important to understand what takes place as the puppies begin to live outside in the warm, wet world of the uterine horns and in the busy world of people and other animals. The first need of the newborn is heat. Without it, the puppy will die, and thousands of puppies die each year because the bitch's owner did not realize the importance of adequate heat for the whelps.

Generally speaking, during the first week of life the puppies require temperatures ranging from 85° to 90°. The second week, a temperature of 80° is necessary. By week three, the puppies can thrive in normal room temperature providing they have the dam's heat to keep them warm and they are protected from extremes in weather conditions. In every case, a thermometer should be used to monitor the temperature.

Providing auxiliary heat, when needed, can be tricky and the concept should be understood thoroughly before attempting it. Since the puppies need to live in an atmosphere of higher than normal temperture, a heating pad or heat bulb will be necessary. The location of the auxiliary heat source in relationship to the puppies is what's important.

If the heat source is placed far away from the dam, the puppies will seek it out and leave the dam's side for the comfort of the heat. When the heat source takes the puppies away from their mother, they do not get the proper nourishment. Ideally, heat and nourishment should come from the same source, the dam. Therefore, by placing the heat source near the dam, she can feed the litter, and they can keep warm at the same time. The auxiliary heat should be removed as soon as possible to encourage the puppies to stay close to their dam.

Care and Nutrition of the Dam

The dam should be allowed many opportunities to stretch her legs and relieve herself during the time she's actually nursing the puppies. Because she will be consuming a much greater quantity of food and liquid, her eliminative needs will rise drastically. It is likely that for the first few days to a week, she will be most reluctant to leave her family to urinate or defecate. In that case, it is the owner's responsibility to insist that she get some exercise. Within a day or so after whelping, she will learn that, once she's been taken outside, the sooner she does her business the sooner she will be allowed to return to her puppies.

In addition to exercise and periodic trips for elimination purposes, she should be kept clean. Again, books on whelping give specific instructions on this matter and should be followed. Clean mothers are inclined to raise clean puppies.

Proper nutrition for the dam during lactation is critically important. The dietary needs of the nursing mother will depend on several factors, such as the size and general condition of the litter. For example, a large litter made up of strong, aggressive puppies will drain a dam considerably. Therefore, the dam should be fed food that is marked "complete and balanced" in the amounts she desires. She should be given several (three or four) meals a day rather than one large meal simply because her stomach can't hold her total daily requirement of food. In addition, she should receive fluids to augment the solid food and there should be fresh, clean water available to her at all times.

The books we've listed in the bibliography give excellent instructions on nutrition for lactating bitches. Dr. Collins offers the following advice.

59

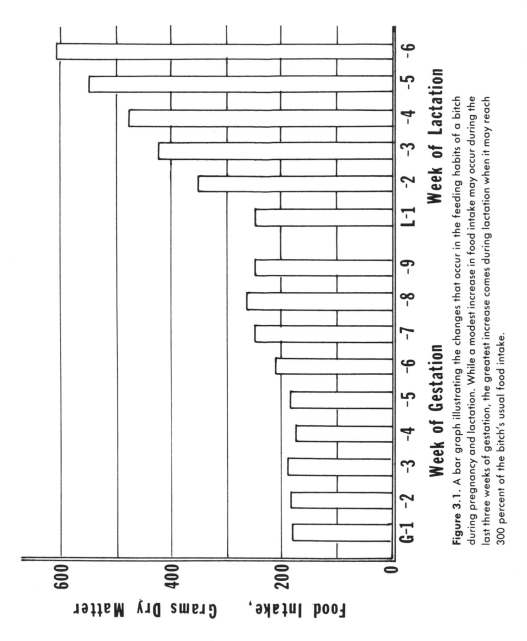

Figure 3.1. A bar graph illustrating the changes that occur in the feeding habits of a bitch during pregnancy and lactation. While a modest increase in food intake may occur during the last three weeks of gestation, the greatest increase comes during lactation when it may reach 300 percent of the bitch's usual food intake.

Nutrition During Lactation

Malnourishment of the bitch during lactation causes the unnecessary death of hundreds of pups every year. To the dog feeder who is also a dog breeder, understanding this single fact and knowing what to do about it can make the difference between operating in the red or the black.

Most nutritionists agree that lactation is the most critical nutritional stress encountered by a bitch. By the time the pups are four to five weeks old, the bitch will require two-and-one-half to three times the amount of energy and nutrients every day that she required before she became pregnant (see Figure 3.1).

By keeping an accurate weight chart of a bitch prior to conception, during pregnancy and during and after lactation, it is a simple matter to determine how her body weight at weaning compares to her body weight at conception. Bitches that are fed properly during pregnancy and lactation should not lose more than about 10 percent of their body weight during reproduction. This is one of the most critical tests that every dog feeder can use to test the adequacy of a diet.

An inadequate diet during lactation is most likely to appear as:

1. Lactation failure (agalactia). This is a complete failure of the mammary glands. The bitch produces no milk at all from which the pups can be nourished. These pups cry continuously, fail to gain weight and, unless immediate remedial feeding is started, will die.
2. Lactation depression (dysgalactia). While the mammary glands are functional, they're unable to produce adequate amounts of milk to fully support the pups' complete nutrient needs. The pups are restricted in growth rate and may become stunted.
3. Deficient milk. The milk, although it may be produced in adequate quantity, is deficient in one or more nutrients.

Many bitches will consume little or no food for the first 24 hours after whelping. If a bitch remains inappetent longer than 48 hours after whelping, consult your veterinarian. Between the two of you, you should be able to determine the cause of the lack of appetite. Persistent inappetence following whelping usually signals serious complication of pregnancy or whelping—complications that can lead to grave consequences unless attended to early.

61

Under healthy circumstances, the bitch's appetite will increase sharply following whelping. This increase will continue until the puppies are weaned, or until supplemental feeding is begun. By the fourth week of lactation, the bitch's intake will have doubled over the amount eaten during gestation.

One of the most frequent causes of lactation failure is the refusal of a dog feeder to provide adequate quantities of food for the bitch. Another common cause is feeding a diet intended for maintenance use. This becomes especially disastrous if the maintenance diet is marginal to start with. Even with adequate maintenance diets, gestation produces depletion, lactation produces deficiency. Reproductive failures may also be caused by foods containing nutrients of poor digestibility, even when they are fed in increased amounts. In both of these cases, the bitch often is incapable of consuming enough food to obtain all the nutrients and energy she needs.

The ideal reproduction diet is one that can be fed both during pregnancy and lactation. This poses certain problems, however. An adequate diet for a healthy bitch during pregnancy does not need to exceed that of a high-quality maintenance diet. Such a diet used during lactation may fail completely, however. This failure is due to the fact that even high-quality maintenance diets are not concentrated enough. The lactating bitch will require three times more nutrients and energy at the peak of lactation than she required during maintenance. But, many lactating females cannot, physically, consume three times as much food. Even when they can, eating such large quantities reduces the digestibility of what they do eat to such an extent that they are still unable to obtain all the nutrients and energy they need.

A satisfactory diet for lactating bitches should contain about one-and-one-half to two times as much energy and nutrients as a high-quality maintenance diet. This means that a diet suitable for raising rapidly growing puppies is also suitable for feeding lactating bitches. It also means that lactating bitches that are properly fed will need to eat only about one-half again as much as they would if being fed a maintenance diet.

If ordinary commercial dog foods are used for a reproduction program, certain modifications will probably be necessary. During pregnancy, the commercial food may be entirely satisfactory if it is balanced and contains sufficient calories to maintain the bitch's weight. During lactation, the addition of three tablespoons of corn oil to each pound of dry food, or one tablespoonful to each pound of canned food, will improve the caloric density of the food. A similar quantity of chopped, raw liver should also be given when the food is being fed to a lactating bitch.

As lactation progresses, it will become necessary to increase the number of daily feedings to reduce the quantity of food the bitch must eat at any one meal. Smaller meals at more frequent intervals help to avoid the discomfort and loss of nutrient digestibility caused by larger meals. By the sixth week of lactation, it is not unusual for the bitch to be eating three times what she was eating during gestation.

The ideal goal for a reproducing bitch is to have her weigh within 10 percent of her prepregnancy weight after her puppies have been weaned and she has completely stopped lactating. This occurs only rarely, unfortunately. Even when recommended feeding practices are followed during pregnancy and lactation, many bitches will deplete some of the reserves in their bodies.

Dam's Care of the Puppies

How the bitch cares for her litter will have a profound effect on the ultimate outcome of the puppies. Newborn puppies do not relieve themselves without stimulation. As the dam feeds her brood, she will also use her tongue to stimulate the puppies into relieving themselves. The dam also does all the cleaning up by consuming the excrement, so there are few if any droppings to mess the den area. During the Neonatal Period, or until the puppies open their eyes and begin to walk, the dam will see to it that the nest remains fairly clean, but the owner must still change the bedding daily.

Dogs are instinctively clean animals and do not dirty their sleeping quarters. As the puppies' eyes open and they begin to get up on their legs and walk, they will begin to eliminate on their own. At that time, most puppies will seek the farthest area of the nest to relieve themselves. Many times, a bitch will allow her two- and three-week-old puppies to wander away from the sleeping area, relieve themselves and she will then go over to the area when they finish and partially clean up the droppings.

It isn't until the owner begins to offer the puppies supplementary feedings that the dam will stop cleaning up after her puppies. Once they begin to eat on their own, they will nurse from her occasionally, but she will stop stimulating the puppies altogether.

Other behaviors of care will be keeping the puppies close to her and thwarting the wanderer who finds itself far from the nest area. When they eat, she will lick their faces and keep them generally clean. And all the while, she will be interacting with them as they grow and learn about their new world.

Housing

The original whelping box is usually quite adequate for the first weeks of the puppies' lives. It provides sides so they can't fall out, protects them from drafts and helps to keep in the heat they require. Some whelping boxes are designed with a railing around the inside so the bitch cannot accidentally roll on a puppy and kill it.

The box should also provide some sort of opening so that the dam can go in and out at will. There will be times when she needs or wants to get away from the puppies and this special entrance can keep them in while she goes out.

During the Transition Period, however, they will begin to investigate the opening and eventually find their way out, at which point a suitable second home will be required. It can be a simple matter of adding higher sides to the original box, or moving the dam and litter to a larger area where they will be safe. For example, many breeders transfer them to a corner of a laundry or utility room in which they have built a wired enclosure. By making one of the wire sides higher than the puppies yet low enough for the dam to jump over, the puppies can be safe and confined while the mother has the freedom to come and go as she wishes.

Cleanliness

In the Neonatal and Transition Periods, keeping the puppies clean is done by the dam because the nerves that control the puppies' evacuation don't develop until the puppies are three to four weeks of age. Although there are occasional instances when a dam will refuse to care for her puppies, most bitches do a fine job of caring and housekeeping during the first 20 days of the puppies' lives. Since the dam manages the puppies' elimination, the nest remains fairly clean. However, clean bedding must still be put down every day for general sanitary reasons. By following this regimen of daily cleaning, the chances of infection will be minimized, and there'll be little or no odor from the litter area.

64

The bitch should be kept clean at all times. With long-haired bitches, this may mean keeping her mammary glands and anogenital area washed frequently, as the long hair attracts and holds debris and secretions, both of which cause unpleasant odors and can lead to bacterial infections.

Comfort

Generally, if the bitch is warm and comfortable, her puppies will be, too. When the mother is content, she will feed and interact with her puppies in a relaxed state. Her feeling of well-being will, in turn, be sensed by the young, and they will stay close to her and nurse freely.

If a bitch is uncomfortable with her environment, she will attempt to change it on her own. If her attempts to move the puppies to a more suitable place are ignored, she will persist and spend most of her time carrying them from one place to another, thereby neglecting the important tasks of feeding, cleaning and keeping them warm. Of course, in situations such as this, the puppies are the ones who suffer the most.

Sometimes a bitch will try to tell the owner prior to whelping that a chosen area is not suitable. If this happens, the easiest way to determine a better location for mother and babies is to watch the dam. By consistently going to a certain area and trying to make a nest by digging, the dam is saying that she wants to whelp and raise her puppies in the place she's chosen. In most cases, the owner can then arrange things to satisfy both dam and owner.

Keeping the nest area warm, dry, draft-free, clean and secure is the key to comfort. When sufficient thought has gone into the preparation of the nesting area prior to whelping, then there will be little to do once the bitch and owner get busy with raising the litter.

Litter Size

The size of the litter can have a profound effect on the kind of dog a puppy turns out to be. For example, if a puppy is an only puppy, it will grow up never knowing how to get along with other dogs for it will never have the opportunity to interact with dogs of its own age and size. (See the special section at the end of this chapter for more on one-puppy litters.)

On the other hand, a puppy that grows up in a large litter will have many experiences in learning how to cope with other dogs. It will learn how to establish social relationships with other dogs and how to inhibit its aggressive behavior to assure its own survival. Throughout that learning process, it will discover where it fits in the scheme of the pack.

Sometimes a litter is so large that the owner has to divide the litter and let the dam care for one-half at a time. I have a friend who had a bitch that whelped 14 healthy puppies. The lady kept seven puppies in a heated whelping box and tube-fed and evacuated them part of the time while the bitch nursed the other seven. Then, at the next feeding, my friend switched puppies so the dam had the first group to care for until the following feeding. All 14 puppies survived and were extremely healthy and well adjusted (probably due to frequent handling!). However, this type of situation calls for a most dedicated breeder who is able and willing to stay home and provide all the extra care necessary.

In most cases, however, nature plays the role of selective reproduction. Most bitches have the number of puppies they can raise. We must remember that, in the wild, only the normal healthy ones would survive. If the dam couldn't care for all the puppies she whelped, the weaker ones would succumb. This process of elimination is the basis of the survival of the fittest.

Interaction with Dam, Sire, Other Animals

The puppies begin interacting with the dam right from the moment of birth. Instinctively they seek her for warmth and sustenance. In turn, she feeds them, cleans them, licks them to evacuate both bladder and bowel, stimulates them and provides the warmth they require.

Shortly after birth, sometime between five and ten days of age, the puppies become more sensitive to scent, touch and temperature. For the first ten days of life, the puppies nurse and cling closely to the dam for survival. At this stage, they can tell, even though their eyes have not yet opened and they can't walk, where their mother is located in the nest. They can smell her, they can feel her and they can tell by temperature awareness how close or far away from her they are.

The first social relationship of their lives has begun. The strongest alliance, that of care giving, begins with the dam. In the neonatal puppy, this relationship begins the development of behavior that will grow and change with the dog for the rest of its life.

This German Shepherd Dog puppy has just had its face cleaned by its sire. Allowing interaction with their sire, if possible, is extremely beneficial to the puppies.
—*Charlotte Schwartz*

A typical litter of English Setter puppies.   *Percy T. Jones*

In most breeding situations, the sire of the puppies does not have an opportunity to interact with his get. Many times the sire lives hundreds of miles away from the dam and litter and he never sees them once the mating is completed.

In a few cases, however, the breeder will own both the dam and the sire. How and when the sire gets the opportunity to interact with the puppies is frequently decided by the owner. Sometimes a sire will not accept the puppies and present a threat to their safety and survival. Other times, he will begin interacting with them much as my friend's dog does right from the days when they are in the whelping box.

As the puppies grow and begin to venture beyond the limits of the nest, the dam will visibly withdraw her initial constant vigilance and allow the sire to assume more and more of the responsibility of interaction with them. And as he does, he will begin teaching them things they will need to know as adults. He will allow play fighting and investigative behavior, but only to a point. Severe infractions of his invisible guidelines will bring on heavy, but harmless, consequences. At this stage in their lives, the sire's disciplinary actions are usually more bark than bite. And the smart puppy gets the message loud and clear.

When there are animals in the neonatal puppies' environment other than their dam or sire, they quickly learn to accept them, too. Often a breeder will have several other dogs, perhaps a cat or two, or any of a number of other pets. The only time this situation might present a problem is in the case of the one-puppy litter. Without the opportunity to develop social relationships with its littermates, the puppy will make attachments to the other animals that can affect its ability in later life to get along with other dogs. For instance, many singleton puppies have grown up with a cat in the house and, as adults, relate well with cats yet cannot tolerate dogs.

A well-balanced assortment of other animals in the neonatal puppies' environment does not appear to adversely affect them providing the other animals are healthy and react neutrally to the puppies. Of course, the dam will usually determine which animals can and cannot interact with her litter and at what point they will be allowed to try. It is advisable to let her set the rules since, at this stage, she knows infinitely more about her young and their care than humans do.

At least for the first ten to 14 days, most bitches will not allow any interference with her litter either from other animals or strangers. And when you think about the capabilities of the puppies at such an early age, there is little interaction possible since the puppies are so helpless in this stage of development.

Interaction with Humans

The neonatal puppy is so immature and underdeveloped in almost every sense that it is virtually immune from psychological stimulation by humans. There is little value in human contact at this time since it can't see or hear, it lacks the motor skills necessary to function on its own, and its intellectual capacities have not fully developed.

Several scientific studies have been done with neonatal puppies to find out if human contact or lack of it during this period would have an influence on the later development of the puppies. In each study, it was learned that the primary need of neonatal puppies is the care they receive from their dam and little else matters.

Most breeders will pick up each puppy at least once a day to move and examine it. This certainly can't hurt the puppy providing it's gently done and for a very short period. Most of the time, the dam will be watching carefully while this handling is going on. Once the nest area has been cleaned and the puppies have been returned to the dam, she will proceed to lick them and gather them to her breast for nursing.

Litter Socialization

Until the puppies' eyes open there is almost no socialization between them. This sightless period lasts until they are between ten and 13 days old. The range of variation for the opening of the eyes is due to breed and individual causes. Some breeds open their eyes by the time they are ten days old, yet others open theirs at 12 days. Then, of course, there is frequently a particular individual in any litter whose eyes don't open until a day or two after its littermates. This variation can be caused by the fact that the puppy was not as mature at birth as the rest of the puppies in the same litter.

Although we cannot actually define sleeping as socialization, the only behavior with physical contact between two or more individuals in the Neonatal Period is the sleeping habits. Since the puppies cannot control body temperature until the end of the

Transition Period, they seek the warmth of each other when they sleep. Thus they arrange themselves into a pile whenever the dam is away from them or whenever they are cold. This habit of piling up on each other provides them with maximum heat at times when the ambient temperature falls below their need.

During the latter part of the Transition Period, puppies begin to interact with each other in very simple and clumsy ways. They become vaguely aware of each other and will occasionally start to mouth or paw at one another. This is the beginning of play learning and doesn't become intense until after they are 21 days old. The dam is still the primary need in their lives, and they respond in unison to her presence.

Early Nerve and Muscle Development

During the Transition Period, from 13 to 20 days of age, the nerves and muscles mature and signal the onset of great physical changes and resulting behavioral developments. Actually, the greatest change in nerves and muscles occurs when most puppies are 18 or 19 days of age, and it is usually so dramatic that they seem almost to be different animals from one day to the next.

Temperature control and metabolism are now developed. The cerebral cortex in the brain matures so that they can see, although visual perception is not quite fully developed yet. Their ear canals open and they can hear.

The final stage of hindquarter development begins and they can stand and crawl backwards at about 18 to 22 days of age. Their attempts at walking are, as in most animal infants, halting at first and frequently result in toppling over. Once they're on their feet, tail wagging begins but it remains insignificant until they are more conscious of others in their environment. It isn't unusual to see a 20-day-old puppy standing alone and wagging its tail.

A puppy in the Transition Period shows a startle to sound response by 20 days of age and a more pronounced response to physical stimuli by 21 days. The brain is quite well developed by 21 days.

Sucking muscles in the mouth grow stronger and the puppy can lap milk from a bowl, although it can't chew solid food as yet. The nerves that control evacuation are almost fully developed, allowing the puppy to begin leaving the nest area to eliminate. This behavior doesn't become well established until the puppy is between three and

70

four weeks old, so its attempts to keep the nest clean are often feeble, but it tries. And as long as the dam is feeding the puppy, she continues to clean up after it.

As we can see by this discussion of the state of being of the puppy at birth and how that state changes within a short 20 days, it becomes easier to understand how vital it is to provide the best possible environment for the development of the puppy. When some aspect of the birth environment is lacking, it will alter the outcome of the puppy as it matures into a dog. Take, for example, the puppy that is taken from its mother at 15 days of age. The primary social relationship required to give the puppy a stable foundation in dealing with other dogs when it grows up begins with its mother. If she is not present during the Transition Period and later, then the puppy will never be able to interact well with other dogs in later life. This is one of the major causes of dog fighting among adult dogs.

In short, the Transition Period is a period of reorganization of behavior. The puppy goes from a sedentary, helpless creature to one that is becoming aware of its environment with all the ramifications that that implies. It is, indeed, a critical period.

SPECIAL PUPPIES

Occasionally, a breeding will result in an unusual event that will create the necessity for some very special handling by the owner. Such unexpected occurrences as sick puppies, one-puppy litters and orphaned puppies call for extraordinary care and handling, and can tax the owner's time and talents in the raising of the litter.

Sick Puppies

When an entire litter of puppies contracts a viral or bacterial disease or, as in some cases, suffers the effects of a genetic accident, the veterinarian and owner must work together to help the puppies fight the problems and survive. If the initial symptoms of trouble are ignored by the owner, it may be too late for the veterinarian to save the puppies by the time he or she finally gets to see them.

In most cases, the litter owner will have the first opportunity to see signs of trouble. Symptoms such as vomiting, diarrhea and the resulting dehydration, fever and crying are some of the more obvious signs. In addition, the dam may behave in an unusual manner toward the puppies in question. Sometimes she will push them aside and refuse to let them suckle. This is a sure sign there's trouble in the whelping box!

Prompt attention by a veterinarian can frequently save an entire litter, but not without the full cooperation and help from the owner. Therefore, puppy owners must be constantly alert for anything out of the ordinary within the litter, either in one puppy or all of them.

Once the problem has been identified, the veterinarian will supervise the feeding, medicating and general care of the sick puppies. Wise owners will follow his or her instructions precisely.

The One-Puppy Litter

A one-puppy litter is another kind of problem. Initially, the puppy usually does very well, growing fat and friendly because it has its mother's milk all to itself and the owner's attention in an inordinate amount.

However, as the puppy grows it has no littermates with which to interact. It never learns that someone is probably bossier than he or she is, and that others may be more submissive. Although the puppy has plenty of interaction with its mother, it grows up thinking it's top dog on the totem pole, except for mother.

When a puppy such as this leaves its birth environment and faces the big world of other people and dogs, it's in for a rude awakening. And therein lies the problem.

Since this puppy never had the opportunity to play and learn from its own peers, it will not know how to interact with other dogs. This can lead to aggression and dog fighting or the reverse, a fear of other dogs that stresses it so severely that it cannot function when in the company of other dogs.

Remember, the period from 21 to 35 days is the litter socialization period in which the puppy develops its ability to interact peacefully with other dogs. Denying a puppy this experience of living and playing with littermates will result in lasting effects on the puppy (see Chapter 4, Interaction with the Pack, for more details).

Sometimes the owner of a one-puppy litter can locate the owner of a litter of puppies of similar age and size. Once those puppies are weaned, it may be possible to introduce the single puppy into that litter for the purpose of interacting with them, either by living with them or visiting on a frequent and regular basis. Even a few hours a week of socialization with a normal-sized litter of puppies can prove to be a tremendous advantage in helping the single puppy learn about the world of dogs and how it fits in. Once again, the advice of the puppy's veterinarian should be sought and followed before attempting this.

Orphaned Puppies

Fortunately, orphaned litters are infrequent, but every once in a while, a dam will die or become sick and unable to nurse and care for her puppies. In these cases, it becomes the sole responsibility of the owner to feed and care for the puppies.

By referring to the Development Chart on pages 172–75, one can easily understand how helpless newborn puppies really are. Add to that the loss of their dam and the problem becomes a life or death matter. There are, however, ways to raise such puppies and this special section offers methods and considerations that have been proved successful by experienced breeders in overcoming the loss of a brood bitch just when her unique expertise was needed the most.

This is not a time to panic. Rather, it is a time to calmly evaluate the situation, consider how many puppies must be cared for and the manner in which each will receive the attention required for survival. The critical elements of survival are heat, housing, nourishment and evacuation. Last and most importantly one must decide who in the household is going to be responsible for the puppies' upbringing. With newborn puppies, this can mean a full-time job—yes, 24 hours a day—simply because puppies that are hours old need to be fed and evacuated every two hours. Therefore, it is best accomplished by two or more people so that no one person has total responsibility. After all, humans need to sleep, too.

Tube feeding is probably the easiest and most efficient method of providing nourishment of the right kind in the correct amount to each puppy. Instructions for tube feeding and formulas for newborn puppies are comprehensively given by Dr. Collins at the conclusion of this section (see Feeding Orphan Puppies). Now, let's consider the specifics of temperature, housing and evacuation.

Temperature Control

Puppies from birth to seven days need to be protected from drafts and in an atmosphere that is 90° Fahrenheit. From eight to 14

The door of this whelping pen allows the dam to leave the puppies when she wants to get away from them, yet the Dachshund puppies are safe within. —*Karla Martin*

The white spots on the chests of these Bedlington Terrier puppies will not be obvious when the coats have cleared to mature color.

days of age, they should have a room temperature of about 85°. By the time they are 15 to 21 days, they do best at a temperature of 80° and then it can be lowered to 75° for the period of 22 to 28 days.

Two efficient ways of providing heat for newborn puppies are by utilizing electric heating pads and heat lamps. There are, of course, cautions in both methods.

Electric heating pads concentrate the heat in one spot and can dehydrate and/or burn the puppies if the pad is not well covered with toweling. When raising a large litter, using more than one heating pad will allow all the puppies room to find warmth without smothering each other.

A heat lamp can be arranged to hang directly over the whelping box, thereby affording a wider distribution of heat. The desired temperature can be maintained by raising and lowering the lamp.

In either case, a cooler area around the edge of the whelping box will give the puppies a place to go if they do not feel comfortable in the center.

The most important thing to remember when providing artificial heat for newborn puppies is that the temperature must be monitored at all times. A regular household thermometer should be kept in the whelping box and adjustments made so that the temperature remains constant. When puppies get too hot or too cold, their own body thermostats are forced to work overtime or simply aren't well enough developed to regulate their internal temperature. That, in turn, burns up vital body energy needed to help them grow, thereby robbing them of optimum development, or it kills them.

Housing

Housing for newborn puppies is basically very simple. They do well in wooden or cardboard whelping boxes with sides to prevent them from falling out. Toweling, carpeting, blankets or any soft fabric is ideal for bedding. Newspapers, although easy to change frequently, are slippery and cause the puppies to slide as they move about the whelping box. The traction provided by fabrics helps them move about—remember, they can't walk yet. If cut-up pieces of an old blanket are used, the pieces can be changed daily and laundered.

Ideally the whelping box is near the heart of the home and its activities, yet not in the path of household traffic. Since the puppies will need to be monitored almost constantly, it is much easier to keep an eye on the litter when those responsible don't have far to go to check on the puppies' well-being.

Having the litter in a barn, garage, basement or isolated laundry room is, first, inconvenient and, secondly, not wise. Too many things can go wrong—a puppy gets "lost" in a cool corner and can't find its way back to the litter, the temperature changes unexpectedly jeopardizing the puppies, etc.

Evacuation

At birth the puppies' nerves that control evacuation are not developed enough for them to urinate and defecate by themselves. The dam must help them or they will die. Eliminative behavior does not develop until the puppies are three weeks old.

In the absence of the brood bitch, the owner can do this for the puppies. The process isn't difficult—the only difficult thing about elimination with newborn puppies is remembering to do it often enough. When you realize that a litter that lives with its mother is constantly cleaned and licked by her you get some idea of how often she tends to each puppy. And, by some method known only to herself, she seems to know exactly which puppy has been evacuated and which hasn't at any given time!

After each feeding and after a reasonable sleeping period, each puppy should be picked up in your hands. Take a piece of soft tissue or a cotton ball and dip it into tepid water. Then gently rub the anus and the vulva (vagina) or penis of the puppy. With most puppies, you will notice them urinating and defecating almost immediately upon feeling the stimulation of the warm, wet cotton or tissue.

To keep track of each puppy's elimination, place the puppy in a separate box alongside the whelping box after it evacuates. When all the puppies have been evacuated and are in the holding box, then return the entire litter to the heated whelping box.

It's also a good idea to keep a chart and record the results of each puppy's elimination every time they are evacuated. By doing this, a puppy that isn't evacuating as it should, i.e., it fails to defecate or urinate as often as the others, can be singled out and watched more closely in the future. Sometimes puppies become constipated or develop diarrhea, which could be symptomatic of other problems or sickness.

A word of warning: Without human assistance in evacuating, orphaned puppies will probably not survive. Each time the puppies

76

are fed, the digestive process begins all over again thereby causing the need to evacuate. Every time the puppies become active they also need to eliminate. Failing to do so, they soon develop uremic poisoning or the bowels become so compacted that the puppies weaken and die.

Managing an orphaned litter is made easier by arranging a schedule that includes monitoring the temperature in the nest, feeding and evacuating the puppies, and keeping the whelping box clean. I have raised two litters of orphaned puppies and, with a little help from family members, was soon able to tend to the needs of the puppies while maintaining a reasonable schedule of my normal activities.

It took a little juggling, but the demands of the puppies soon became so apparent that we could anticipate, within minutes, when it was time to feed, evacuate and tidy up. The best way to tell if a litter is doing well (and if you're doing a good job of foster-mothering!) is to observe the puppies.

A healthy, happy litter will sleep piled on top of each other for several hours at a time, evacuate regularly with your help and exhibit a general air of contentment. There will be little or no crying, except perhaps just prior to feeding time, and they will occasionally almost sound like a litter of kittens with the soft little grunts and groans they make. One thing for sure—if they're well fed and well cared for, you'll know it!

Feeding Orphan Puppies

The first thing to do in any puppy feeding program is to weigh each puppy. A record of this weight and the date it was taken should be kept on a separate record for each individual. The second thing is to determine the diet to be fed and the quantity of food needed to start the program.

The ideal food to feed newborn puppies is bitch's milk. Any replacement for bitch's milk should approximate it as closely as possible. A suitable emergency formula can be made from evaporated canned milk by mixing three parts of evaporated milk, as it comes from the can, with one part of warm water and adding one-quarter teaspoon of powdered dicalcium phosphate to each cup of the mixture.

Far more convenient are the commercial formulas designed to be used for feeding orphaned puppies.

No matter how closely a formula resembles bitch's milk, there is one ingredient that the dog feeder cannot provide—colostrum. Colostrum is found in the first few days of a bitch's milk and protects her puppies from disease while their tiny bodies are learning to protect themselves. There is no substitute for colostrum. Whenever possible, every newborn puppy should nurse a newly freshened dam for at least 24 hours, even if the dam is not the puppy's own.

To determine the daily quantity to feed each puppy, the following calorie intakes for preweaning puppies should be used:

Weeks of Age	Cals./lb. body wt.	Cals./oz. body wt.
1st	60	3.7
2nd	70	4.4
3rd	80–90	5.0–5.6
4th	90	5.6

The total daily quantity a puppy requires can be divided into four to six equal feedings that will leave the puppy with a moderately distended stomach following each feeding. The exact quantity to be fed must always be left to the discretion of the person feeding the puppy. Start with the figure given as a guide to estimate the quantity needed, then let the puppy tell you how much it really needs.

A puppy tells a dog feeder whether it is receiving too much or too little food in several ways. One of the most often recognized, but least likely to be accurate, is crying. Hungry puppies do cry, but so do cold puppies, hot puppies, puppies just disturbed from a nap, lost puppies, unhappy puppies, etc. Anything that makes a puppy unhappy will probably also make it cry, even having its tummy too full.

The reaction of the puppy's system is the most accurate gauge to whether or not it is getting enough to eat. Every time you feed a puppy, two things should happen. The puppy should have a bowel movement and it should urinate. Sometimes a puppy may need a little encouragement by rubbing its anal area (see Evacuation), but it should always perform both acts if everything is going correctly.

A puppy's stool should be formed as it is expelled, but its consistency should be soft and pasty. Its color may vary from a pale tan to a mahogany brown. The inside may be yellow-brown. Stools that are green, bluish-white or clear signal trouble. Stools that are watery, lumpy, hard or curdled may also indicate that something is wrong. Whenever either off-color of off-form stools occur, stop feeding immediately and skip the next feeding entirely. Begin the following feeding with a formula that has been diluted one-half with boiled water. Continue to feed the same quantity as you did the undiluted food. If this fails to produce an improvement in the stool, cut the quantity you are feeding by 25 percent at each feeding. If stools continue to deteriorate, call your veterinarian.

The quantity of urine should be about the same each time and the color should be pale yellow to almost clear, never deep yellow or orange. It should always be like water and never like syrup. If the urine is scanty, dark in color or syrupy, it usually indicates that the pup is not receiving enough water. Additional water should be supplied, either added to the formula or fed separately. If the urine seems excessive in amount, unduly clear or thin, the water concentration of the formula should be reexamined to make certain that too much water is not being given. If urine production stops altogether for longer than four feedings, take the puppy to a veterinarian promptly.

Bottle feeding. Bottle feeding newborn pups is not much different from bottle feeding any other newborn mammal. First of all, everything should be impeccably clean. The bottles and nipples, themselves, should be sterilized, the formula fresh and hands and utensils washed in hot, soapy water.

Pour just enough formula into a bottle to provide a single feeding and warm it to room temperature. This can be done by holding it under hot tap water, while turning the bottle. Do not use a boiling water bath because it overheats the tiny quantity of milk.

Hold the puppy in a normal upright position and poke the nipple into its mouth. Some pups will get the hang of it immediately. Others are less perceptive. Squeezing a little drop of milk onto the tip of the nipple before putting it into the pup's mouth may encourage some pups to start sucking on the nipple.

Never squeeze milk out of the bottle while the nipple is in the puppy's mouth!

Use a separate bottle for each pup. There are three reasons for doing this. First, you know precisely how much you are feeding to each pup and can measure precisely how much that pup drinks. Second, if you get a disease outbreak, you reduce greatly the chance of spreading it from puppy to puppy with an unclean nipple. Third, if you need to go back and try to get a pup to drink a little more, you don't need to keep close track of how much each pup has already eaten. The amount any pup still needs is what's left in its own bottle.

If a puppy gags or strangles and milk starts coming out of its mouth and nose, take the bottle away immediately. Place the pup between your palms, head outward, and use your fingers to hold its head and backbone in a straight line. Place the pup at arms length and swing it up and down. The centrifugal force will sling the milk out of the puppy's mouth and nose and, with luck, out of the windpipe as well.

Tube feeding. The feeding tube eliminates bottles and nipples that have to be cleaned after each feeding and sterilized before the next.

The equipment needed is quite simple. It consists of a #8 or #10 French infant feeding tube, a hypodermic syringe and a substitute for bitch's milk.

Once the proper equipment has been accumulated, determine the proper depth to which the tube should be inserted by measuring, on the tube, the distance between the puppy's nose and a point just behind the elbow; this is approximately where the stomach of a puppy lies. Mark the tube at the correct depth with a marker or piece of tape.

Grasp the puppy firmly with the opposite hand, placing the thumb and forefinger on the cheeks, one on each side of the puppy's mouth. Gentle pressure is placed on the sides of the mouth and, at the same time, the jaw is pried open with the little finger of the hand holding the tube. By maintaining light pressure, the mouth can be held agape once it is opened. Into the open mouth, insert the end of the tube over the groove formed by the top of the tongue. Cautiously push the tube back into the pharynx. Push the tube straight in, to the depth of the predetermined mark. If it is accidentally inserted into the trachea, healthy puppies will cough and struggle violently. A tube that is inserted into the trachea will usually stop about half-way short of the mark.

Once the tube is successfully inserted to the depth of the mark, slip your thumb and forefinger from the cheeks to the tube, and hold it firmly in the mouth at the level of the mark. With the tube thus firmly in place, place the open end of the tube between the forefinger and middle finger of the hand that holds the tube in the puppy's

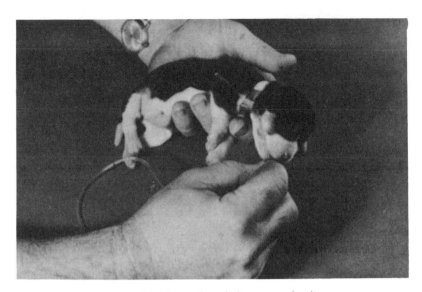

Measure the tube and mark the proper depth.

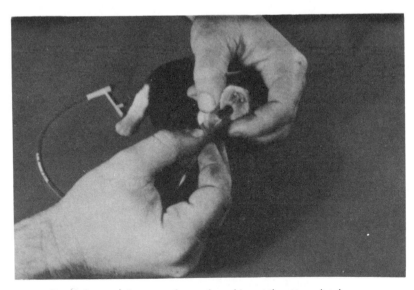

Carefully open the puppy's mouth and insert the stomach tube.

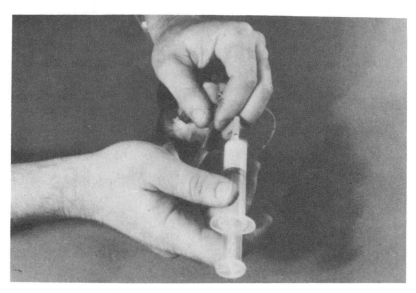

Connect the syringe to the stomach tube.

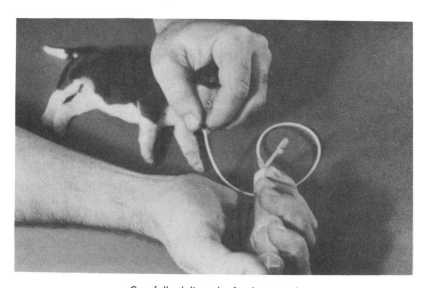

Carefully deliver the food material.

82

mouth, as shown in the photo. Pick up the previously filled syringe and insert it snugly into the open end of the tube.

Slowly apply pressure with the thumb to the syringe plunger and deliver the substitute bitch's milk. Continue to deliver the food until the correct amount has been administered. Draw back slightly on the plunger and gently slip the tube out, still attached to the syringe.

At about three to four weeks of age, as soon as their eyes open and they are able to move about with some ease, it is time to begin teaching tube-fed puppies to eat from the pan.

4

Litter Socialization Period: 21 to 35 Days

W E MOVE NOW INTO another critical period: the Litter Socialization Period. As the name suggests, it is the beginning of the puppy's first awareness of another living being other than its mother. How it reacts to and with its mother and littermates will determine what kind of an individual it will be for the rest of its life.

Will it be a friendly dog? A bossy dog? A fear-biter? A leader or a follower? All these questions will be discussed and examined in this and the succeeding chapters. In addition, we must look at some further physical and mental developments, all of which are leading us to the total puppy and ultimately the total adult dog.

The Litter Socialization Period occurs at from 21 to 35 days of age. Some of the behavior and development that begins late in the Transition Period continues, bringing the puppy even closer to the adult stage. In other aspects, new behavior begins as the nerves and muscles continue to develop. In other areas, there are still more developments required before the puppy will be able to function and survive on its own.

The Senses

During weeks three and four the brain, nerves and muscles make further strides toward the total development so that, now, the puppy begins to develop conscious perception and control of its movements. In other words, the puppy becomes aware of its environment and begins, however haltingly at first, to respond to what it sees, hears, feels, smells and tastes. Initially the responses are extremely elementary, but the fact that the puppy demonstrates awareness of things going on around it shows us that it is, in fact, growing up.

For example, during the Neonatal Period and well into the Transition Period, the puppy did not respond to the arrival of its mother simply because it couldn't. It just lay there in the nest and waited for her to come to it.

Now, with conscious perception, the puppy sees the dam approaching and physically attempts to go to her for nurturing. Although its legs remain wobbly, it will voluntarily move toward her along with the other puppies, who frequently bump into one another and topple over several times before they reach her. It may even utter a little squeaking or mewing noise in welcome. This kind of response is typical of a three-week-old puppy.

As the Litter Socialization Period proceeds, the puppy gains strength and dexterity. By the end of the period, it walks quite well, begins to run and can back up. This seemingly simple behavior, however, involves development of the brain, the nerves and the muscles. A lack of proper maturation in any of these areas would prevent the puppy from taking the appropriate steps of development toward maturity.

Although the puppy's ear canals opened during the Transition Period, it isn't until the Litter Socialization Period that the brain develops auditory perception. Because a puppy's motor skills are also developing during this period, it begins to respond to what it hears. While this is happening, the startle response mechanism of the brain is reaching maturity so the pup now responds to sudden noises.

In addition, the puppy begins to experience emotional reactions to things and events in its environment. Consequently, sudden unexpected noises can startle and frighten the puppy. Therefore, care must be taken to assure a secure and constant environment. For example, a puppy born in a whelping box in the kitchen will grow up with the noise of a household so that loud, kitchen-type noises will not frighten it. On the other hand, a puppy raised in the relative quiet of an outdoor kennel or isolated store room would react to the

Learning how to cope with life beyond the period with the dam and littermates is the purpose of the Litter Socialization Period. This Norwich Terrier is just about ready to go out and conquer his world. —*Robert Congdon*

Researchers and behaviorists have determined "critical periods" in the juvenile development of dogs. Knowing when they occur and what they involve is important to both breeders and new owners.

startling noises of pots and pans if it were suddenly moved into the kitchen of an active houehold at this time in its life. In other words, the puppy becomes acclimated to its birth environment and usually adjusts well to moves providing the change occurs gradually over a period of a few days.

Another aspect of development that ties in with the brain is the maturing of the vocal chords. The puppy can now bark. Levels of excitability usually determine a breed's predisposition to the habit of barking. Some breeds are more vocal than others and seem to use this form of communication more freely than the quieter breeds. Sight hounds, for example, are usually quiet even as adults, whereas terriers vocalize about everything.

Since the temperature control and metabolism functions of the brain are mature by the end of the Transition Period or the beginning of the Litter Socialization Period, sleep habits change. No longer do the puppies lay in a pile. Instead, they lay side by side when they sleep.

Finally, maturing of the eliminative muscles during this period gives the puppy total voluntary evacuation. At this stage, all the puppies in the litter leave the nest area to eliminate. Since most breeders begin offering food to supplement the bitch's milk, the bitch stops stimulating them to evacuate when she is not actually nursing them. Initially, they wander anywhere to eliminate, but as they mature they begin to prefer one particular area, and they will urinate and defecate every hour or two until they are 12 to 16 weeks old.

At this point the breeder becomes totally responsible for keeping the litter and their living quarters clean. Failure to do so can cause disease and force the puppies to develop undesirable eliminative habits.

As was pointed out earlier, dogs are instinctively clean animals and do not normally soil their sleeping quarters. By forcing puppies to live and sleep where they evacuate, they will ultimately become "dirty dogs." Consequently, diligent cleaning habits by the breeder are essential from this point on.

Awareness

Now that so much physical, mental and emotional development has occurred, the puppy enters a new realm of behavior. The puppy's new awareness opens up a world of fascinating things and places to explore.

At first, the puppy plays by itself, exploring various areas of its living quarters, its own body, a shadow on the wall, a littermate's tail. It chews on things partly because its first teeth have begun to emerge and partly as a social, investigative behavior. Frequently, it can be found chewing on a littermate while a third one is returning the favor! This initial chewing is mostly painless and serves to satisfy curiosity regarding littermates.

A puppy's newly developed investigative behavior will also allow it to wander away from the nest, but the dam is usually quick to retrieve the pup if it goes too far. Generally, the puppy will venture only a short distance so that it can still see and hear its littermates and the nest.

Interaction with the Pack

During the Litter Socialization Period, the puppies spend a lot more time interacting with each other than they previously did. Without realizing it, their first informal lessons in living have begun. The behavior is mostly limited to play within the nest area.

Despite the fact that early interaction between the puppies is limited due to their own physical limitations, it is extremely important that there be interaction between them. This early behavior teaches each puppy about the hierarchy of the social order in which it lives.

The puppies' play periods teach them a great deal about who's who in the pack. It sorts out the leader, the followers, the dominant and the submissive individuals. A puppy's first experience with learning to control its own actions for the benefit of the pack comes during the latter part of this period. In addition, the puppy begins to learn that it must inhibit its aggressive behavior in order to remain a welcome member of the pack. The results of these lessons produce lasting effects on all the puppies.

As the puppies in a litter begin to experiment and establish the order of dominance within the pack, certain individuals begin to assume the leadership roles. For example, in a mixed litter where there are male and female puppies, usually the largest male puppy becomes the dominant one. In an all-female litter, size is frequently not the deciding factor. Rather, it appears that vocalization and sometimes a combination of size and vocalization determines which bitch puppy becomes the leader.

In cases where a breeder decides to keep a puppy from the litter,

This German Shepherd Dog puppy is learning that his father will play with him if he drops his front end to the ground and wags his tail. —*Sue Hill*

It is important for all puppies to accept handling from an early age. This also facilitates veterinary attention and grooming. In breeds where trimming is necessary, as with these Sealyham Terriers, the ease of handling is even more essential. —*Tauskey*

that puppy will never grow up to realize its full potential if it is not separated from its dam sometime between eight and 12 weeks of age. Living with its mother beyond this point removes the need to develop emotional stability and the puppy frequently becomes a shadow of its mother rather than a distinct individual of its own. Keeping it away from its mother from the age of eight weeks to approximately 16 weeks, offering it lots of human socialization and new experiences, and treating it as if it were an only dog in the home will enable the puppy to develop fully and become a well-rounded adult dog. Once the sixteenth week of age has passed, it can return to live with its mother with no ill effects. They will simply treat each other as two unrelated dogs, often the mother being dominant over the puppy simply because she is the older one.

During the latter half of this period, the first signs of agonistic behavior can be observed. Because it can growl and bark, voluntarily move its limbs and control the movement of its head and mouth, the puppy begins to grab something and shake it. Often it will grab a passing littermate's tail or an ear and shake it violently as the victim screams to get free. This is practice for prey-killing and, if the puppy were a wild dog, would serve the dog well in hunting with the pack.

Because man has domesticated the dog, we must understand this behavior and find substitutes during the development of such traits. A few soft rags or rubber toys can serve the purpose well. Certainly, trying to deny the puppy the development of such an instinct would create massive behavior problems later on in life.

During this period, a puppy's relationship with its dam becomes more complex. Whereas in the beginning she provided the puppy with care giving and nursing, she begins now to discipline the puppy as well. A typical scene of dam-puppy interaction would portray the puppy biting the dam's tail as she lays cleaning him. Suddenly, he begins to bite her foot, whereupon she will look down at him, growl very softly and nudge him.

If the puppy ignores the warning growl, the dam will take further action to stop the puppy's behavior. She may growl more seriously or, more likely, put her mouth around the puppy's head and pull him away. If the little fellow persists and returns to chew on her foot, she will grab him and growl fiercely. She does not inflict injury to her young one, but she does discipline the pup until such time as he indicates by his behavior that he understands her and accepts her authority over him.

As we can see, the Litter Socialization Period is a period of discovery for the infant puppy, a time in which it learns all about the other dogs in its litter and initiates experiences with adult dogs, beginning with its mother. It's easy to see, then, how critical it is for the future of the puppy to get off to a good start by having meaningful learning experiences. The single puppy would not have the opportunities to interact with littermates that the puppy born into a litter has. And, as we shall see in the next few chapters, this interacting grows with the puppy and becomes even more significant as it gets older.

Eating Habits

In this period the puppy begins to eat semi-liquid food, due to the emergence of its first teeth. When the puppy is ready, the dam will frequently introduce it to food by regurgitating partially digested food.

The uninformed breeder will usually look aghast the first time this happens and think the bitch is ill. But, in the wild, this is the method used by the mother and other adults in the pack to carry food from the hunt back to the puppies.

Once a breeder understands and expects this behavior, however, it's fascinating to watch. Usually the dam will have been away from the puppies for a while. Upon her return, the puppies will all approach her and lick her face, particularly in the region of the mouth and lips. This is called care-giving solicitation and it is simply the puppies' way of asking their dam to feed them. Frequently when this happens, the dam will contract her stomach muscles and regurgitate a pile of semi-soft food, at which point the puppies will eat vigorously.

In addition to this feeding habit of the dam, she also changes her nursing position. Instead of laying on her side for the puppies to nurse, she stands, usually stimulating and cleaning them as they nurse in this new position. By standing for the nursing process, the dam is preparing the puppies to become independent of her and eat on their own.

The dam should not be hurried to wean the puppies at this time because, as she's feeding and interacting with them, she is teaching them invaluable lessons they need to survive. For example, the dam will often discipline the overly greedy puppy so that it learns to take its fill yet not prevent the others in the litter from eating their share, too. If this puppy was not disciplined early in life by its dam, it might grow up to become the type of dog that cannot be approached while it is eating. This, of course, can be extremely dangerous if there are young children or elderly people in the household. Such a dog would also react with equal aggression toward other pets in its adult home, thereby making it almost impossible to live with harmoniously.

The supplemental food offered by the breeder as the puppies are being weaned should be of the highest quality and in the amounts and number of feedings best suited to that particular breed. Chapter 6 of *The Collins' Guide to Canine Nutrition* gives detailed instructions and should be studied carefully prior to the time when the dam begins the weaning process. As the dam weans the litter, her own nutritional requirements will change, too. Dr. Collins also gives specific information regarding how to feed the brood bitch at this time. A summary of his instructions are given here for quick reference.

Weaning Procedure

The weaning procedure accomplishes four things. First, it teaches the puppies to eat solid food. Second, it allows you to feed the puppies a food more satisfactory for them than the food you are feeding their mother. Third, it begins the social interaction between puppy and man. Finally, it allows you to reduce the bitch's intake of food at the same rate you increase her puppies'.

The ingredients that make up the food fed to a weanling puppy must be highly digestible. An excellent weaning diet can be easily made by preparing a slurry using one of the specialized dietary animal foods designed to be fed to patients with gastrointestinal disorders, mixed with equal parts of the bitch's milk substitutes. Top-quality, ration-type, canned commercial foods also make satisfactory solid foods to mix with the liquid part of the diet. In all cases, one-quarter to one-half tablespoonful of grated, raw liver should be added to each can of food just before it is mixed. The slurry can be either beaten with a fork or mixed in a blender. For the larger breeds, it may become economically necessary to use the higher quality, expanded dry foods in combination with the canned foods to blend with the liquids.

Teaching the young puppy to eat from the pan can be a hilarious experience. To some dog feeders it may also seem like a time-wasting step in rearing a dog. By individually hand-training each pup, however, you can assure yourself that no pup will fall behind nutritionally simply because it doesn't know how to eat food from a pan.

Place the pup up to the pan of food and stick its muzzle in. Try not to get its nose in too, if possible. I've never strangled a puppy this way, but some of them really splatter and fuss when that milk hits them in the face for the first time!

Some puppies get the hang of pan-feeding almost immediately. One lick of their tongues and they are after the milk mixture like it was their first meal in a week. Other pups may appear to miss the idea entirely and would rather bathe in the pan than drink from it. After a few minutes, or before your patience has become exhausted, pick the puppy up, wipe off the surplus milk with a damp cloth, dry the dampened hair and put the pup back with its littermates. Then try another, until every pup in the litter has had a turn.

Once you have succeeded in training one or two pups to become proficient eaters, it may help to put a slow-witted pup up to the bowl with one of the good eaters. Puppies learn by example, and since an empty stomach is one of the greatest motivating forces known to animaldom, the "see and do" method often works well.

As the quantity of food consumed by the puppies increases, the quantity of food being fed to the dam should be decreased by an equal amount. By the time the pups are separated from their mother, she should be eating about the same quantity she was eating before she whelped.

Whatever the weaning mixture used, the quantity of milk substitute should gradually be reduced, so that by the time the puppy is six or seven weeks old, it is eating only solid food. At this point the puppies should be separated entirely from their mother, and weaning is complete.

Interaction with Humans

This is the first time in a puppy's life that it becomes aware of humans. Usually the first people it will get to know are the owners of the dam, or the breeders. Many times, the breeders are a family with children who have bred, perhaps for the first time, this particular litter of puppies of which our puppy is a member. Let's examine some of the experiences and reactions of the puppy as it becomes aware of the human family. In order to do that, we must return to the day of the puppy's birth.

You will recall that the puppy was born with only the sense of touch and taste and a very elementary sense of smell. It could neither see nor hear. During those early days, its mother provided all its needs automatically without it having to do anything. Human socialization was not needed since he was incapable of conscious perception.

However, the breeder *was* involved with the puppy right from the start as the breeder assisted at the whelping and helped the dam keep the nest area clean. Ideally, the breeder picked up each puppy in the litter at least once a day and examined it and moved it about in the cleaning process. As time wore on and the litter entered the Transition Period, the puppies began to see and hear the people around them. It wasn't until the Litter Socialization Period, however, that they became really aware of people and they demonstrated this awareness by responding to the humans.

As the people in a puppy's life become more important to it through the process of care and supplemental feeding, the puppy makes the association that people are good to be with.

The puppy in the Litter Socialization Period needs an unaltered environment. Therefore, a puppy's experiences with people should be short, pleasant and always within the confines of the pup's environment. Taking the puppy away from its nest, dam and littermates should be done only if absolutely necessary and for very short periods. Remember, the puppy at 21 to 35 days of age is still not ready to begin life as an individual. Rather, it needs its littermates and familiar surroundings plus limited human contact in order to function and grow. Disturbing this process and rushing independence will thwart development later on and can leave a puppy with undesirable neuroses as an adult.

Although the puppy's brain has made remarkable strides toward complete development, a puppy cannot remember anything until it is 21 days old. In fact, the puppy's memory span will not be mature until the puppy is 35 to 36 days old. Therefore, trying to teach the puppy a behavior during this period is futile and can cause severe problems later on.

For example, if a person tried to teach a puppy to sit before the memory span had developed, the person would likely become frustrated when it appeared that the puppy wasn't learning. In his frustration, he might yell at or hit the puppy and would probably exhibit a certain amount of nervous tension. The puppy, in turn, would pick up the person's reaction and respond fearfully to the entire situation and the person. In other words, the lesson would become a negative learning experience for the puppy.

It is far better to wait until the puppy is physically, mentally and emotionally ready to learn before attempting to teach it anything. In the next chapter, we will discuss learning in detail. But, for now, it is important to know that the critical lessons of learning how to get along with other dogs are the main function of the Litter Socialization Period.

Because dogs are highly social beings, it is possible to achieve such successful human interaction.
—*Wilbur Boone*

The celebrated entertainer Betty White getting cozy with some Samoyed puppies. Dogs with sound temperaments that have been properly socialized, like these, will take handling in stride.

5

Human Socialization Period: Weeks Five to Twelve

IN EACH PERIOD of the puppy's development we have seen crucial changes occurring that constitute the metamorphosis of a puppy into an adult dog. As we observe these changes, we become aware of the simultaneous development of the brain, body, emotions and intellectual ability of the animal. And we begin to realize that although physical development will one day be complete, the behavior of the dog is not fixed. It will be constantly changing throughout the life of the dog.

The fact that the puppy will someday leave its mother and littermates to take up its life in a human pack makes the Human Socialization Period the most important stage in the puppy's development to us, the humans. The experiences the puppy has during this period and the changes that occur as a result of those experiences are the responsibility of all the humans with whom the puppy comes into contact—breeders, new owners, veterinarians, groomers, kennel workers, pet shop employees, instructors of puppy training classes and anyone who has anything to do with the puppy. Consequently it behooves all of us, whenever we find a puppy in our midst, to know precisely how to interact with the puppy so that it gets the most out of the occasion.

Since the new owner's involvement with and responsibility to the puppy are so complex, two chapters have been devoted to this subject. Chapter 6 discusses the new home environment while Chapter 8 details the specific requirements of the new owner.

In this chapter we will learn how the puppy views the people, places and events within the realm of its new awareness. We'll examine how these experiences create lasting effects on the dog.

Declaration of Independence and a First Fear Period

By 28 days of age, the puppy's ability to learn has just begun and its emotional stability is established. While neither of these aspects of the brain have completed maturity at this time, the puppy is capable of learning simple things by the age of four weeks.

Seven days later, when the puppy becomes five weeks old, we see the emergence of curiosity and investigatory behavior. In addition, the puppy's startle response to sudden, unexpected movements and sounds develops. Thus emotional reactions to things that frighten the puppy can be observed. Since this is also the time when the dam is weaning the pups, the fear of strangers also becomes evident. However, this early fear period usually passes quickly because the puppy is developing so rapidly and learns not to respond to irrelevant stimuli—providing those sounds, movements and people did not prove threatening when the puppy first noticed them. But this is not the only time in the puppy's development that it will experience a period of fear. It will go through another fear period at age eight weeks which we will discuss later in this chapter. A third one will occur in the juvenile stage.

At this tender age our little friend is not ready to go far afield (and won't be until approximately 12 weeks of age), but the urge to investigate things just beyond easy reach grows stronger every day. Witness a litter of puppies at five weeks of age and no doubt you'll see one or two of them climbing up to look over the sides of the whelping box. If you observe quietly for another few minutes, you'll probably see one of them lift itself so high above the edge that it falls out onto the floor. Breeders love to brag about "the first puppy out of the nest" because they feel that usually indicates a brave little fellow who will become a leader in the future. I'm not so sure he'll become a leader, but I think it's safe to assume he'll be the most inquisitive one.

At any rate, the puppy is beginning to recognize that there is, in fact, a world beyond the nest. The development of its brain, nerves and muscles provides the puppy with the ability to react to this exciting new world. Further, its newfound exploratory ability will bring the pup into contact with other people and other animals— and how it perceives them will determine what the puppy will be like for the rest of its life.

Socialization and Chewing on People

A puppy's experiences with people during this critical period of human socialization will establish, for all time, how it sees people in general. For example, if a puppy is subjected to a houseful of screaming, stomping children who race around it, handle it roughly and otherwise make it react in frozen panic or flee to the safety of a dark corner, it will forever be wary of children.

If, on the other hand, the children have been taught how to be gentle, to use soft tones when speaking and to avoid overwhelming the puppy, the puppy will associate children with pleasantness in the future. Playing with a soft toy, having a game of chase on the lawn and having moments spent in gentle loving will serve to create a bond of trust and friendship between dog and children that will last a lifetime.

The adults in a puppy's world should be gentle, firm, kind and never threatening. Standing over it and yelling "NO!" as it chews on forbidden objects or circles in preparation for eliminating on the carpet are counterproductive actions and detrimental to the puppy's development. In addition, these behaviors do not serve to teach the puppy that it must not chew on the furniture or relieve itself in the house. (Chewing on forbidden articles and housetraining are addressed later in this chapter.)

What the puppy does need at this point in its life are pleasant experiences with all humans to show that people are nice and to be trusted. The puppy must feel it belongs, no matter how many humans will eventually make up the pack. Socialized correctly, the puppy will quickly learn that humans, like its mother, are care giving, loving and maintain a leadership role.

At this point in time the puppy begins to stay awake for longer periods and transfers its habit of playing with littermates to playing with humans. In the context of puppy/human play, it is again learning. For example, a puppy begins to carry objects in its mouth and, if lucky enough to live with people who can think as a puppy does and have educated themselves regarding puppy development, this new behavior of retrieving and carrying will be reinforced as a rewarding activity because it pleases the human companions.

In contrast to learning positive things to do with humans, a puppy also investigates the possibility of chewing on people (hands, feet, arms, ankles). At this age a puppy's gums hurt because of teething and the soft, warm flesh of human beings is ideal for sinking those needle-like teeth into. Furthermore, many people insist on keeping their hands in front of the poor fellow's face either to control him or get his attention. Moving hands and wiggling fingers on the hand and face area only serve to incite the puppy's bite reflex thereby compounding the problem. Is it any wonder, then, that the puppy chews on people?

This behavior is a lot easier to prevent than stop once it gets started. Chewing and biting are undesirable habits, no matter how young the puppy may be. And, what's worse, it never gets better. There's an old saying among dog people that "puppy chewing for teething turns to biting for blood."

If people allow a puppy to chew on them when teething, isn't it reasonable to assume that this puppy will one day chew on them to relieve frustration when it doesn't want to do something it's told to do? All breeds of puppies chew when they're teething and all breeds of dogs can bite when they're frustrated, angry or afraid.

In the following section of this chapter we will discuss in detail the method used to teach a puppy about the hierarchy of its new world and its place within it. Once a puppy learns that all the humans in the pack are leaders and that he is a follower, the puppy will accept that role and be content.

By providing the essentials of a meaningful relationship with a dog during its socialization period of development, behavior problems as an adult can be avoided, thereby creating a lasting bond of peace and harmony within the pack. Consequently, for optimum results in human socialization, the puppy must associate all humans as pack members who fill physical, emotional and intellectual needs and are not threatening to safety and survival.

Socialization with other animals began long before the seventh week of life. Remember how the puppy began learning from its dam and littermates when just three and four weeks of age? If the association with other animals continues during this period of five to 12 weeks, the puppy will be able to interact peacefully with animals as an adult.

100

German Shepherd Dogs, who are reportedly sheep killers, can be taught to herd flocks of sheep and protect lambs from wild predators if the dogs are raised with sheep from an early age. Recently, I had a Labrador Retriever in a class who loved other dogs, all cats and goats. When I asked, "Why goats?" the owner explained that the Lab had grown up in a large paddock with a nanny goat and behaved as if the nanny was her mother!

Expecting an adult dog to cohabit peacefully with cats when the dog didn't see its first cat until it was two years old is asking for trouble. Most dogs just can't do it. I'm sure there are certain dogs within certain breeds that can learn to tolerate cats, but I wouldn't want to try it with any of the hunting, working or terrier breeds or any dog with a high-intensity prey instinct. Chances are good that it would end in tragedy, particularly for the cat. Therefore, it seems prudent that when a puppy is brought into a home, careful planning should be made to assure that the puppy learns, right from the beginning, that it must live in peace with all other animals. If the owners intend to acquire a cat, bird or hamster in the future, it behooves them to get the puppy used to other pets during this critical period.

Order of Dominance

The following is an article that appeared in the November 1985 issue of *Off-Lead Magazine*. I wrote it to explain the importance of establishing an order of dominance in a household with one or more dogs. It gives directions on how to perform the Dominance Down, an ideal way for people and puppies to build that all-important bond together.

Occasionally, a person will have an older dog that is just too big and too strong to put down on his side. In cases such as this, where a dog has never been shown who his leader is (oftentimes dogs like this think *they* are the pack leader!), a substitute behavior—the Stand-over—can be used effectively.

While the dog is standing, straddle him with one leg on either side of his body. Place your arms around the chest, right behind the front legs, and lock your fingers together under his chest. Now lift the front legs off the floor gently and hold for about one minute. If the dog struggles, say "No!" sharply and, placing one hand on the scruff of the neck while maintaining the other hand beneath the chest, shake him as you repeat the verbal warning.

As soon as he quiets down, release and tell him he's a good dog in a soft tone of voice. Repeat the Stand-over daily for a week and after that whenever he's misbehaving and you want to let him know that his behavior is unacceptable to you. Always end with softly spoken praise and a pat.

Whatever method you use, Dominance Down or Stand-over, it is absolutely essential that the dog understands that it is a member of *your* pack and you (and all humans) are the leader. Like the Cocker Spaniel in the following story, the dog won't care what number it has in the pack—all that matters is that it has one.

EVERY DOG NEEDS A NUMBER

Once upon a time there were two dogs, a Cocker Spaniel and a German Shepherd Dog, who lived next door to each other. In each of the dogs' houses there also lived a man, a woman and two teenaged children.

One day the dogs were talking to each other over the fence in the backyard. The German Shepherd was looking very glum that day, and the Cocker Spaniel asked him what was wrong.

"Oh, I don't know. I just can't figure out my pack. One day the man lets me sleep on his bed and tells me how handsome I look lying there with my head on his pillow. The very next day, when I lie on his bed, he comes into the bedroom and screams his head off at me. The next thing I know, he grabs me and when I growl at him, he thrashes me. Yet sometimes, I growl at the woman and she just leaves me alone—says I'm becoming mean. I'm confused," lamented the German Shepherd.

"Do you ever get confused in your house?" he asked his friend.

"My goodness, No!" said the Spaniel. "What's your number anyway?"

"What do you mean 'What's my number?'" asked the Shepherd.

"You know, your number. For example, my man is Number One, the woman is Number Two, the children are Numbers Three and Four and I'M NUMBER FIVE," explained the Spaniel, emphasizing the "Number Five." "Isn't that great? It's wonderful to be Number Five!" she added, puffing herself up with pride.

The German Shepherd looked at his small, blonde friend and envied her such an important position in her pack. He wished he had a number and could be just as proud as she. But instead, he lowered his head and mumbled ever so softly, "I don't have a number. Nobody ever gave me one. How did you get yours?"

"Oh, I've always had Number Five, ever since I came here. I hardly remember how they gave it to me, but every once in a while, when I get too excited or noisy or whenever one of my pack thinks I'm being naughty, they remind me of my number. Then they always tell me how wonderful I am to be Number Five."

The little Spaniel lowered her sultry eye lids, wiggled her whole bottom and, with a self-assured twitch of her stubby tail, she pranced back toward her house. As she left, she said, "I hope you get a number someday."

With that, the handsome Shepherd went over to lie in the shade of a big maple tree and think about the conversation he'd just had with his friend next door. He wished he could talk so he could ask his family pack for a special number, too.

This little vignette is, of course, fiction but the message it portrays is proven fact. Pack animals such as dogs (and man) can only exist and flourish in a social group which has a clearly defined hierarchy. And without the harmony which a hierarchy creates, the species cannot hope to perpetuate. In other words, the structure of an order of dominance in any social group insures its survival.

In the example above, the Cocker Spaniel will live out her life in peace and fulfillment providing she continues to accept her number and is content with it. To her it is not important that she is Number Five: it only matters that she *has* a number. The only exception to this would be if she were unfortunate enough to live in a household where the humans made her Number One. In that case, she would fail because she would be incapable of making decisions and being responsible for the welfare of a pack of humans.

The case of her friend, the German Shepherd, is another matter, however. Apparently, the social structure of his household is rather loose. Sometimes he's Number One in the hierarchy, sometimes he's Number Five, and I'd bet money that there are also times when he fits somewhere in between.

The fact that he's allowed to lay on his master's bed doesn't necessarily mean he's Number One. Nor does the fact that his master removes him from the bed make him Number Five. But when he growls at his mistress and she walks away from him, he *thinks* he's dominant over her. However, from his conversation, one gets the idea that he doesn't always growl at her. That's the crux of the problem. And it creates a very dangerous situation for his entire pack.

When any individual in a social group does not clearly understand and accept a specific place in that society, it can mean trouble. And this "learning one's place" occurs in dogs as early as 12 to 16 weeks of age.

A litter of puppies, for example, begins to interact with each other by the time they are 21 days old. By three months, the puppies have developed a strong tendency to dominate each other. They bite, chew, growl, pounce and play fight. Through play fighting each puppy learns who it must submit to. There is rarely bloodshed and severe injury, but there is a lot of ritualized behavior as each puppy learns to inhibit its aggressive tendencies and get along with its peers. Frequently, the largest and heaviest dog becomes the leader, Number One, and the others take up positions beneath him.

When a puppy goes to a new home, it needs to reestablish its position in the new pack. It's at this time in the puppy's life that knowledgeable owners help the puppy to make a smooth transition by showing it where it fits in the order of dominance in the new pack. In other words, it needs to be assigned a number.

Without the opportunity to interact with its own species when it is very young (before 16 weeks of age) and with man as it gets older (from seven to 20 weeks of age), the puppy may grow up to be hyperaggressive. It seems the puppy that's been denied the opportunity to learn about social order at an early stage finds accepting a position in any hierarchy later in life difficult if not impossible. These findings have been proven by many scientists and behaviorists over the last forty or so years.

Finally, when a puppy enters the developmental stage of sexual maturity, he usually exhibits a resurgence of social dominance. In short, he attempts once more to climb the hierarchy ladder and dominate all those in his pack. If the owners are not aware of this behavior and the reasons for it, the dog can reach the top, or leadership level, with disastrous consequences.

For example, an overindulged dog may assume a dominant role in the household. And the dog which is confused about its position in the hierarchy—one day he's "top dog" and the next he's "low man on the totem pole"—will become frustrated. Then the owners must deal with another problem, that of frustration-aggression.

However, knowledgeable dog owners are not only aware of

the sexual maturity stage in the dog's life, but they know how to handle him so the dog will remain in his rightful position. Providing the dog is a normal individual and the maturity development stage proceeds without complications, the dog will remain a stable member of the social pack in which he lives.

How can a person tell, short of being bitten, if a dog is acting in a submissive or dominant manner? In his book *Understanding Your Dog,* Dr. Michael W. Fox presents a list of behaviors which indicates dominance and submission by dogs. Here are some of the most common behaviors:

DOMINANT BEHAVIORS

Stalking
Growling, snapping, biting
Baring teeth to reveal incisors and canine teeth
Assumes "T" position with head over submissive dog's neck
Pushing with shoulder or hip
Walking around dog, stiff-legged, head and tail held erect
Stands on subject's back
Pushes dog down and stands over submissive dog

SUBMISSIVE BEHAVIORS

Lowers front part of body, tail tucked under
Allows dominant dog to place feet on its back
Retracts lips horizontally—raises forepaw
Licks face area of dominant individual
Tail between legs, ears back, directs gaze away from dominant dog
Rolls onto back, remains still
Urinates, defecates
Sits or lies down and flexes hip to expose inguinal (groin) area

These behaviors are ways in which dogs, using their bodies, speak to each other. We call it "body language." And for dog owners to live in harmony with canines, we should become familiar with and learn to use it.

The best example of this Dominance-Submissive sequence can be found between a dam and her puppies. Whenever a puppy behaves in a manner which is unacceptable to her (for instance, the puppy wanders away from the nest), she will go over to him, put her mouth over his head, and her paw on his back. When he's down, and possibly screaming as though he were being murdered, he will eventually relax under her paw. When the puppy no longer resists, the dam will remove her paw and walk away, sometimes eliciting a period of play from him.

Once an owner understands that his own body language speaks more clearly to his dog than any verbal language (dogs aren't born knowing how to understand words), then the owner can let the dog know he loves him, will assume responsibility for his welfare (dogs want a leader), and what position the dog must assume in the owner's pack. (Remember, man has brought canines into his domicile—dogs did not bring man into their dens!)

It seems only common sense, then, to use one of the behaviors from the Dominance List to communicate to the dog that his place is beneath that of all the humans in the household. Doing that will achieve two objectives. It will let the dog know who's the boss and it will give the dog a number of his own. (Remember the unfortunate German Shepherd that didn't have a number?)

Making the dog lay down on its side, with its head and hips touching the floor, is an ideal way of communicating to the dog what his position is in the pack. We call this exercise the "Dominance Down."

The easiest way to accomplish a Dominance Down is to get down on your knees. Have the dog stand sideways in front of you. Place both your arms over the dog's back. Now take your two hands and reach over and through the center of the dog's body so that you can take his *inside* front leg in one hand and his *inside* back leg in the other hand.

Grasping both front and rear legs (the ones next to your body), firmly, but gently, pull the dog close to you and slide him down the front of your thighs until he comes to rest on the floor in front of you with his legs facing away from your body.

Next, take the hand that was holding his front leg and place it over his neck. The hand that was holding the rear leg now rests over his top, or outermost, hip. Slowly stroke the groin area inside the top hip and you'll feel him begin to relax. The dog may even lift his topmost leg which is a further sign of submission to you.

It is important when placing the dog on his side to manipulate him smoothly and firmly. Do not slam or throw the dog down—you could hurt him. Do not be hesitant when you begin—this gives the dog time to resist you. Simply grasp his legs and, in one fluid motion, lower him to the prone position in front

106

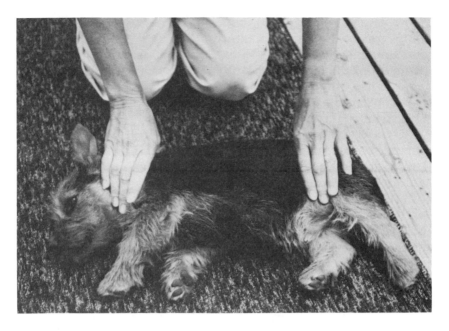

The Dominance Down is used to develop the bond between the puppy and humans and to teach the puppy that all humans are dominant over him.   —*Charlotte Schwartz*

An eight-week-old Beagle puppy meets an adult Dachshund and a Saluki. Note the submissive posture of the puppy when he meets the big dog.   —*Karla Martin*

of you. Use your upper thighs as a slide to ease the dog to the floor—gravity will lower him down.

Now let's go back to Dr. Fox's list. This time we will study the signs of submissions and look for one or more of them in your dog. He may lift his upper rear leg or attempt to roll on his back. He may even urinate. Whatever sign he gives you, he's saying, "OK, friend, You're the boss!"

Occasionally, a person will own a dog which is naturally very submissive. He may or may not be aware of this. If you do a Dominance Down with just such a dog, you will notice almost immediately how submissive the dog really is to you. In this case, it is usually wise and not necessary to repeat it or it may make the dog even more submissive.

The very dominant individual will most likely resist you. The more a dog resists the Dominance Down, the more determined he is to be the boss. This is, of course, the individual who most needs this exercise because man cannot live harmoniously with a dog which dominates him and all the other humans in a household. We simply cannot tolerate a dog running a human pack!

If the dog fights the Dominance Down by squirming, kicking, even screaming, you must react the same way his mother did. Growl at him. Don't yell, "No! Stop that!" or "Lay down!" He won't understand and, furthermore, the panic in your voice will surely tell him that he's getting the upper hand.

If you growl with a deep, emphatic voice, he'll get the message. Continue to hold him down with whatever force is necessary and show him (don't tell him!) that you mean what your body is saying.

Just as the puppy responded to his mother's Dominance Down, your dog will eventually cease his resistance. You'll feel his whole body begin to relax under your hands. When you do, let him lay there for twenty to thirty minutes without moving and without your hands touching him. If he falls asleep, do not waken him until the time is up.

When you do, tell him, "OK, good dog!" and let him get up. Once he's on his feet celebrate with him, praise him, love him up all the while telling him how wonderful he is. Praise so enthusiastically that he gives you some form of recognition, a lick, a paw, tail wagging. Some behavior which tells you, "I love you and I'm not mad because you made me submit to you."

If you've done it correctly, the dog will not only show you signs of affection, but he'll be more attentive, even more willing and eager to be with you. And you'll have opened a door to a deeper, more meaningful relationship with your dog.

108

For the next week, continue to do the Dominance Down every day for twenty to thirty minutes. A dog that is still fighting the exercise at the end of the week should continue for an additional week or whatever time it takes to make him understand. Eventually, however, even the most obstinate individual will give in and accept your leadership through the Dominance Down.

One thing to keep in mind when you begin this program of establishing your leadership is that if you are working with an adult dog which has either been unsure of his position due to a lack of consistency on your part or one which has simply never been shown his correct position in the hierarchy, you will probably find it difficult at first. Occasionally, I've seen older dogs who had been overindulged all their lives and never came to accept a lower position in the pack.

In addition to the initial one-week period of the Dominance Down exercise, the dog should be made to assume this position whenever his behavior is unacceptable to you. For example, if the dog barks incessantly at the arrival of guests and won't quiet down after you've admitted your friends (and he *sees* they're friendly people—not uninvited strangers), you can regain control very quickly by putting him into a Dominance Down for a minute or two.

If there are children in the home and dinner hour becomes somewhat chaotic as the kids and dog race round the house, have the children sit quietly with a book. (Yes, a quiet "down" with children works wonders, too!). Next, put the dog into a Dominance Down. Within minutes, you'll regain peace and order in the house. In other words, the Dominance Down simply says, "Hey, get a hold of yourself and watch your manners!"

By introducing the Dominance Down to any dog, particularly a puppy or a young adult dog, you'll be giving the dog the most treasured gift a dog can receive. You'll be giving him a number that both of you can live with all his life. Remember, the dog doesn't care what position he has in the pack, providing it isn't Number One; it only matters that every dog has a number.

Experiences

The more experiences a puppy has in this critical period, the better equipped it will be to handle the experiences of life when an adult. And some of the least obvious ones to humans can be the most impressive to dogs. Let's take a look at some of them.

Umbrellas are things we don't think about very much, but the first time your dog sees one, it may panic. Now, at seven to 16 weeks of age, let your puppy see one, smell it, paw it, walk around and investigate it. Then pick it up and hold it over your head, for surely the day will come when you have to take the dog for a walk in the rain and you'll be holding an umbrella.

Bicycles, wagons, lawn mowers, trash cans, rakes, hoses, shopping carts and folding chairs all need to be introduced to the puppy. Vacuum cleaners, telephones, hair dryers, electric shavers, washing machines—any appliance that makes a noise and does something that isn't part of his daily routine can become a monster to a puppy. Introduce the puppy to your home and show him how things function. Let him see that these things are a natural part of his life and not to be concerned over. Be chatty, happy, relaxed and the puppy will pick up your vibes and learn to cope as well as you do.

Take him in the car and praise when you get to your destination. Make the trips short, always make sure he's riding on an empty stomach, and don't coddle him when he becomes alarmed at the sound of the motor or the feel of motion as the car moves. A short trip to the corner and back to the house is a good beginning. Build the length of your trips to driving around the block. By the time he can sit calmly in the backseat for five to ten minutes, he'll be ready to tackle the trip to a neighboring town.

One of the biggest mistakes many people make in training puppies to ride in cars is this: They take them in the car to go to the veterinarian. That's it. Shortly, the puppies begin to associate riding in the car with feeling the sting of immunization needles. No wonder they grow up hating the car! Make car riding fun and exciting and you'll end up with a seasoned traveller who's always first at the car when you get ready to go somewhere.

An effective way of helping the puppy make a good association with car riding is to stop after a few minutes of driving and get him out onto the lawn of a shopping center or park and play ball for a few minutes. Then, back in the car for the next leg of the journey. Soon he'll realize that riding in the car means he's in for a special treat rather than a treatment.

Other experiences such as receiving guests into the home, visiting other people in their homes, learning to interact with children and old people if there are none in the household, and

Puppies should be accustomed to a variety of loud, unfamiliar noises as part of training and socialization. With Sporting dogs such as these Brittany puppies, sound-proofing is preparation for a life as a reliable shooting dog.　　　　　　　　　　　—*Percy T. Jones*

Here the puppy is exploring its environment by the method most natural to Beagles . . . sniffing the ground.　　　　　　　　　　　—*Karla Martin*

learning how to display good manners when meeting people on the street are important lessons that are most effectively learned at this early age. Waiting to teach these things to an older dog whose bad habits are already established and who is well beyond the human socialization period can be painfully difficult if not impossible.

It isn't hard to know what experiences you should give the puppy if you simply think about your lifestyle. Expose the puppy to the same people, places and activities that he will know when he grows up. And be sure to relax and enjoy the introductions as you do. Remember, the puppy will be watching for your reactions to the experiences. If you're happy, friendly and enjoying the experience, the puppy will learn to do the same.

Puppy Testing

The results obtained from testing puppies between 6½ and 7½ weeks of age can serve as highly reliable predictors of what the puppies will be like as adults. The results show which puppies will be dominant, which submissive, which are naturally people-oriented, which will prefer the company of other dogs, as well as many other characteristics. Knowing what type of an individual lies within each puppy can prevent the puppy being placed into the wrong hands and the resultant chaos and unhappy ending that so many puppies suffer.

Despite the name "Test," it does not score puppies for which is the best, worst, biggest, smartest, etc. There are no right or wrong answers in puppy testing, no good or bad puppies. It does, however, give a fairly accurate evaluation of the basic dog within the puppy and helps in the understanding and placement of each puppy in the litter.

Puppies should be tested after they are 6½ weeks old. Testing them sooner will result in inaccurate evaluations as the puppies are not neurologically developed enough. Testing later than at 7½ weeks can bring disaster if the puppy is traumatized when he enters the first critical fear period at about age eight weeks. Even a mildly stressful test during this stage can leave a puppy with lifelong phobias. Testing older puppies may result in inaccurate evaluations because their environment may have already influenced their responses to the tests.

112

The tester should be one who does not know the puppies and has no preconceived notion of what they are like. He or she must be objective and look at the test and resulting scores with impartiality.

The puppies should be tested individually away from littermates, dam and other animals in an area where they have never before been. The atmosphere should be as free of distractions as possible.

Puppies should be tested when they are awake and feeling well, never when sick, tired, newly fed (they will want to sleep then!) or suffering from recently given shots or wormings.

Each test is designed to provide insight into a basic personality trait of the individual. For example, if a test shows a puppy to be strongly resistant to human leadership, such a puppy would make a poor candidate for living in a family with several small children and parents who were reluctant to provide the strong social leadership required by such an individual.

Other tests seek to learn which puppies would make good, independent thinkers who could work on their own and not need the close physical support required by a submissive individual. Still other tests tell us how sensitive to touch and sound a puppy is, and another seeks to define which puppy carries a natural tendency to retrieve. All these behavioral traits are desirable in one or more of a variety of situations where humans acquire dogs to perform certain tasks as part of their companionship role with their owners.

Scoring is done on a scale of 1 to 5, 1 representing no or low resistance and 5 for the puppy offering a great deal of resistance to the activity. For example, a puppy that resists being put down on its side would earn a 5 whereas a puppy that lays quietly with little or no resistance would earn a 1.

In the case of the touch test, a puppy that squeals and wiggles immediately upon feeling his paw pinched would earn 5 and the pup that shows no sign of discomfort would earn 1.

Consequently, you can see that this is the type of test where a total score would be inappropriate. Instead, it is designed to evaluate each puppy's response to each activity and assess what that puppy will probably be like as an adult. In addition, other factors such as physical soundness and basic temperament should be weighed before the final decision to place a puppy in any given home should be made.

In the following section is a test chart showing the purpose and evaluation of each test. It is always wise to get the assistance of an experienced person when learning how to test a litter of puppies. Whenever you're in doubt about the results, confer with knowledgeable people in the field of dog behavior and conformation to clarify questionable results. Obedience instructors, breeders, dog show handlers and some veterinarians who are interested in canine behavior may be able to help you evaluate the results more accurately.

Puppy Aptitude Tests

When evaluating the results of the tests, it is important to consider what role the puppy will play in its adult life with humans who comprise the pack. A dominant, insensitive dog would be a good candidate to work in Schutzhund competition, whereas a happy-go-lucky, submissive dog would best fit into the lifestyle of a busy, outgoing family. A dog used for obedience competition or field trial work needs to be amenable to training and eager to please its master. As stated earlier, there is no good or bad score in this series of tests, merely a forecast of what type individual each puppy will become as it matures. Providing it's had a good beginning to life and a future of proper rearing and training, the puppy will develop into the type of adult the tests predicted it to be.

IMPORTANT NOTE: When performing Elevation, Restraint and Touch Tests praise lavishly after each test to dispel the stress the puppy experiences.

TEST	PURPOSE	EVALUATION
ELEVATION—Hold puppy upside down in both hands supporting head, shoulders and hips away from tester's body. Hold in this position for ten seconds.	To determine how puppy handles physical restraint and being dominated by humans.	No resistance would receive a score of 1, while a great amount of wiggling, squirming, crying or growling indicates strong dominant traits and earns a 5. Varying degrees of either would be mid-range.
RESTRAINT—Hold puppy on its side on floor or ground for ten seconds.	To determine how puppy handles physical restraint and stress of being dominated.	Same as for ELEVATION—the higher the resistance, the more dominant the individual.

TEST	PURPOSE	EVALUATION
NEW FOOTING— Place puppy on a sheet of plastic and observe how it reacts to strange footing. If puppy is accustomed to plastic, use material strange to pup.	To determine how puppy reacts to strange things underfoot in its environment and how quickly it recovers from newness and copes with new situation.	Puppy that sniffs plastic and begins walking nonchalantly is more confident than one that freezes and is unable to either stand up on plastic or walk away.
NOISE—Place puppy on floor and have assistant make a loud banging noise (metal spoons against a metal pan) for ten seconds.	To determine how puppy reacts to sudden unexpected noises.	Puppy that runs away earns a 5. Such a puppy is not able to make quick adjustment to unexpected events and noises in life and needs a stable environment and firm but gentle training to build self-confidence.
TOUCH—Hold puppy and pinch, with graduated intensity, the skin between pads of front paw to a count of ten.	To determine the level of sensitivity to discomfort, which provides insight into method of training the dog should be given for optimum results.	Puppy that pulls paw away or exhibits discomfort at the count of one is much more sensitive than puppy that merely notices a pinch at the count of eight or nine.
COME—Place puppy on floor, step away from it about six feet and call it while crouching down and clapping hands.	To determine how readily pup will come to human when the human acts nonthreateningly.	Puppy that comes readily earns a 1 and demonstrates willingness and desire to be with people. A 5 would indicate a very independent puppy who will require much training for reliability.
FOLLOW—Place puppy on floor and, without speaking to it, walk away slowly.	To determine degree of social dependence of puppy.	Resistance to this test (refuses to follow or goes in opposite direction) indicates a strong-willed, independent individual.
RETRIEVE—Sit on the floor with pup and show it a light-weight toy or crumpled paper ball. Toss the toy about three feet in front of pup and observe its reaction. Excite puppy and urge it to "Get it."	To determine how responsive puppy is to moving objects and its desire to pick up and carry object back to human. This test predicts potentially good workers when retrieving and carrying are prerequisites to the job.	A pup that ignores object or sees it and refuses to go over to investigate it earns a 5. The pup that grabs it and carries it back gets a 1. Willingness to retrieve is highly correlated to dogs that must work with people.

115

The Elevation Test determines how a puppy handles the stress of physical restraint.
—*Charlotte Schwartz*

In the Come Test, the tester crouches down into a nonthreatening position, claps her hands and calls excitedly to the puppy.
—*Charlotte Schwartz*

Early Training: Housetraining and Crate Training

Housetraining a puppy is a simple task when done correctly. The trouble comes when people who acquire a young puppy accept advice from everyone and his brother, most of whom know nothing about canine behavior and have never done it themselves!

There are a few do's and don'ts regarding the art of housetraining and, if followed diligently, will result in success in a few days or weeks at the most.

A puppy needs to eliminate right after it eats, as soon as it awakens, after a play session and whenever it acts unsettled and appears to be looking for a spot in which to relieve itself. It can go many hours while sleeping, but must void every hour or so when awake. It is the owner's responsibility to get the puppy outdoors at each of these times and hourly in between these events. The puppy cannot tell you when it needs to eliminate, but if you take it out regularly the puppy will develop an elimination schedule that is predictable. Once the pup grows up, it will stick to that schedule and remind you of its exercise times.

Feeding the puppy on a regular schedule and taking away its drinking water early in the evening will help the puppy get through most of the night with perhaps only one trip outdoors before morning. Although voluntary eliminative behavior begins at three weeks of age, not until the puppy is well over three months of age will it have total muscle development of the bladder. Therefore, the need to urinate frequently will continue for some time, although the length of time between trips outdoors will increase as the puppy grows.

Do not paper train the puppy unless you want it to relieve himself on the paper for the rest of its life. Make the introduction to the outdoors the day you bring the puppy home and it'll learn quickly.

Do not allow the puppy the "privilege" of total freedom throughout the house. The puppy isn't old enough to handle the big world of a house yet. Remember, up until the time you took the puppy from its litter, its whole world consisted of a small area in one room.

Do take the puppy outdoors, and always to the same location, every hour. Praise the puppy whenever it urinates or defecates in the proper area.

117

Crate train the puppy from the day you bring it home. Dogs are social animals and, in the wild, live in packs. Their home is the hollow of a tree, a small den dug into the side of a hill or some similar area away from threatening elements in their environment. In its den, the puppy feels secure, comfortable and content.

Dogs in the wild never soil their dens. New puppies who are not provided with small dens cannot make a distinction from sleeping quarters and voiding quarters. Thus they urinate and defecate wherever they can.

Providing a "den," or crate, for the puppy tells it immediately that this is its resting area and taking it outdoors frequently provides a distinctly different area for voiding—an area away from its "den." A puppy can understand that arrangement and willingly accepts it because it fits in with the instinctual traits of canine behavior.

Many people feel it is cruel to crate train a puppy. Actually, it is cruel not to! Furthermore, a puppy that is crate trained will stay in its "den" for many hours without getting into mischief, destroying things or becoming lonely and upset from social isolation when its human family has to leave it alone in the house. In addition, this "den" should be the puppy's bed at night as well.

Placing the crate next to your bed at night is an ideal way to acclimate the puppy to its new home. It provides a feeling of security for the puppy, and helps with the housetraining. There should be a soft rug or towel in the crate with only one or two toys. No food or water should be placed inside the crate—ingesting food or water merely serves to start the eliminative process all over again and then nobody will get any sleep.

Because dogs are social animals, the puppy may feel lost and insecure when forced to be separated from you at night. Having the puppy in a crate next to your bed will alleviate the loneliness. When it begins to cry, place a hand down into its crate and reassure it that all is well. Shortly, the pup will lick your hand and go back to sleep. If it continues to fuss, take it outdoors to relieve itself and, without getting involved in a play session in the middle of the night, put the puppy back in its crate and turn out the light. A few nights of this routine and the puppy will sleep through contentedly at your bedside. In the morning (and with young puppies, it can be very early!), take the puppy outdoors immediately upon rising. Once you are up for the day, move the crate back into the kitchen or family room where it will serve as the puppy's den for the day.

Dogs that have been crate trained as puppies are much more socially adjusted within the human pack than dogs who have no clearly defined "den" area which is exclusively theirs. Often, adult dogs (and puppies, too!) will curl up for a nap in their crates with the crate door wide open and without direction from their masters. They simply find the comfort and security of their "dens" more to their liking and fulfilling to their needs than a large space in the family's living quarters.

Finally, crate training a puppy gives the owner a place in which to secure the puppy when he, the owner, cannot be around to supervise. Chewing up shoes, furniture, baseboards, and anything else it can get its teeth into soon becomes the puppy's main activity in life while teething and whenever bored. All of these items are costly to replace and create tension between puppy and owner.

But chewing on electric light cords, TV cables and washing machine and dryer wiring can be fatal to the puppy and potentially dangerous since exposed and short-circuited wiring can cause fires. The crate provides a place of safety for the puppy and protection from puppy teeth to the owner and the home itself. And, once a puppy has learned to love its crate, it will forever enjoy the time it spends in its very own "den."

Seven Steps to Crate Train a Puppy

A dog crate is a rectangular wire cage with a solid floor in it. It should be big enough for the dog to lay down and stretch out or sit up without hitting its head on the roof of the crate. Crates can be purchased from pet shops and supply centers. Purchase the size of crate that the dog will require when grown to save buying more than one. The crate should be placed in an area of the home where the puppy can see and hear the family—the kitchen, recreation room or family room. It should be out of drafts and not touching anything the puppy can paw at or chew on.

1. Place a blanket or towel in the bottom of the crate. Add one or two toys, no food or water.
2. Place puppy in the crate and give him a biscuit. Let him stay in the crate for five minutes and then take him out while offering lots of praise. Stay in the room with him for the entire five minutes.
3. Repeat step 2 several times a day.

4. The next day place the puppy in the crate as before and let him stay there for ten minutes. Do this several times. Never remove him from the crate when he's fussing. Wait until he's quiet, then take him out and praise lavishly.
5. Continue building time in five-minute increments until the puppy will stay in the crate for 30 minutes with you in the same room. Always take him outdoors to eliminate after prolonged periods in the crate.
6. Now go back to the beginning and let the puppy stay in his crate for five minutes with you out of the room.
7. Again build crate time in five-minute increments with you out of the room. When the puppy will stay willingly in his crate (he will probably fall asleep!) for 30 minutes with you out of the room, he'll be ready to stay in it for several hours when you must leave him alone.

The puppy should also sleep in the crate at night. Puppies should never be left in crates for hours at a time during the day. They must get out to relieve themselves, eat (some people prefer to feed their puppies in crates, too), exercise and play.

Finally, a puppy's crate is its den where it learns to feel safe and comfortable. If the puppy makes a pleasant association with its crate, it will always be eager to use it. Remember, the puppy's first home was a small, safe area—the next one should be, too.

Outdoor Runs and Kennels

Fenced runs are ideal for large, active breeds that need and enjoy the outdoors. A dog house in conjunction with the fenced area will offer shelter to the dog in case the owner is not present and the dog seeks it. However, one must be sure that the dog can't climb up on top of the house and jump over the fence from the roof. Placing the house outside the area with only the entrance placed against the fence and an opening cut through the fence will alleviate that possibility.

Digging under the fence must also be guarded against. Many small breeds including terriers and toys will spend their idle time digging and, when the owner isn't around, escape only to be hit by a car or stolen. Digging a trench on the fence line and burying the bottom edge of the wire fencing down about 24″ beneath the ground surface will prevent escape by digging.

Large breed puppies such as this 12-week-old Akita usually enjoy spending time each day in a secure, open-air run.

An Irish Setter litter soberly observing the world from their portable exercise pen. These pens are convenient, inexpensive and a safe way to provide outdoor activity for one puppy or an entire litter.

It should be noted, however, that many breeds just naturally don't enjoy being left alone in outdoor runs. They want to be indoors with the family and are quite content in their crates when left alone. If these dogs are put in outdoor runs for any length of time, they will dig, bark, race around in circles and generally become quite frustrated.

Frequently, in suburban communities, their behavior annoys the neighbors who retaliate with formal complaints to local authorities. Many homeowners have had experience with a neighbor's dog who became a public nuisance and the two neighbors ultimately became enemies. The whole problem can be avoided by housing the dog indoors and supervising it when in the yard.

If an owner purchases a puppy of one of the outdoor breeds, such as the hunting dogs, the puppy can learn that the outdoor run or kennel is its permanent home and become a well-adjusted adult providing the owner is willing to supervise and teach the puppy that the kennel is its home. Insulating and draft-proofing the dog house is essential to protect the dog from cold, damp flooring and drafts. If a puppy arrives in the new home in severely cold weather, it is wise to raise it indoors until the weather breaks and the puppy grows up a bit so it can tolerate the cold nights. Raising the puppy indoors the first winter and then weaning it to outdoor life in the spring will insure the health of the puppy. By the second winter of its life, it will be old enough to accept outdoor living conditions.

The biggest problem with raising a puppy in an outdoor kennel is that the owner often slackens his or her regimen of offering the puppy experiences outside the kennel. This, in turn, can cause the puppy to develop kennelosis, an inability of the dog to function outside its kennel. And once the dog finds life unbearable outside its own immediate living quarters, it becomes so stressed when taken away from the area that it can't function or learn. Unfortunately, kennelosis is irreversible in most cases.

More Play Learning

Memory and the ability to learn are fully developed by the end of the puppy's seventh week. So is its nervous system. At this time it enters the period of play learning with littermates and people, group activities and play fighting.

It learns how to inhibit its bite reflexes with regard to both other animals and humans. It learns to investigte new things in its environment, begins to carry things in its mouth, stays awake for longer periods of time and reaches the optimum period for learning how to socialize with humans.

The puppy that doesn't have the opportunity to learn how to inhibit its natural instinct to bite, for example, may well grow up to be a dog fighter. It can also become so obnoxious toward people that whenever it desires, it bites them. This, of course, would lead to an intolerable situation and ultimately euthanasia for the dog, to say nothing of the damage it can do to humans.

On the other hand, if a puppy isn't given opportunities to investigate its world, it may become an adult who is so frightened of anything new and strange that it can't function outside its own familiar surroundings. Here again, we'd have a dog that could never reach its fullest potential due to emotional stress caused by a lack of early socialization and experience.

Learning all about other animals and people and places is the function of the Human Socialization Period from five to 12 weeks of age. In short, just about everything the puppy sees, hears, smells, tastes, feels and does during this crucial stage becomes a lesson learned. And the results of those lessons serve to mold the puppy into the dog it will eventually become.

Veterinary Care and Immunizations

Just as the gastrointestinal system must learn to digest solid food and the neuromuscular system must learn control before the dog can learn to walk, so must the seven- to 16-week old puppy's immune system learn to protect the puppy from disease. It does so by learning to develop protective substances, called antibodies, against each and every bacteria or virus it encounters. If it produces them fast enough to overcome the organisms, it will not get the disease. Furthermore, the body will remember which antibody to produce should the same organism invade again. This head start is called immunity.

The only immunity a puppy has at birth comes from antibodies in its mother's milk, absorbed by the puppy during the first few days of life. The mother dog can give her puppies only the kinds and amounts of antibodies that she herself has, however. During the first few months of its life, therefore, a puppy may encounter organisms for which its mother had no antibodies and the puppy must learn to produce its own antibodies.

As time passes, the antibodies supplied by the mother dog also disappear and the puppy must develop its own antibodies to these diseases as well. With the dangerous diseases, it is always better to give the puppy immunity ahead of time, before the disease-producing organism invades. The safest way to give a puppy immunity is with a vaccine.

All vaccines work about the same way. The vaccine contains an organism that is identical to the disease organism, but has been modified in some way so that it is unable to produce any disease. It has retained its ability, however, to stimulate the puppy to produce the antibodies that will protect that puppy against organisms that can still produce the disease.

Vaccinations stimulate an animal to produce sufficient quantities of antibodies to protect that animal for a given period of time, often about 12 to 15 months. As the quantity of antibody declines with time, the animal may again become susceptible to the disease. For this reason, a revaccination—or booster shot—is very important to assure continued protection.

Antibodies are programmed to protect against only that one specific disease. Distemper antibodies, for example, will not protect the puppy against rabies or Parvo disease. This is why a different vaccine is required for each different disease.

Today there are six vaccines routinely used to protect a puppy against dangerous diseases. They are:

1. Rabies (RV)
2. Canine distemper (CDV)
3. Canine hepatitis (CAV)
4. Infectious Canine Tracheobronchitis (ICT)
5. Leptospirosis
6. Canine Parvo disease (CPV)

In addition to the above, vaccines are also available for Corona virus infection and Bordetella bronchiseptica, one of the organisms incriminated in kennel cough.

While every veterinarian has his own schedule of vaccinations, they almost all will be some slight variation of the following:

Vaccine	Time
First distemper, hepatitis, ICT, leptospirosis and Parvo	Two weeks after weaning (approx. eight weeks of age)
Second distemper, hepatitis, ICT, leptospirosis and Parvo	14–21 days after first vacc. (10–11 weeks of age)
Third distemper, hepatitis, ICT, leptospirosis and Parvo	14–21 days after second vacc. (12–14 weeks of age)
Fourth Parvo	14–21 days after the final distemper and hepatitis vacc. (14–17 weeks of age)
Rabies Vaccination	Four months of age
All Boosters	One year from date of previous vaccination

In addition to a good immunization program, during their first 16 weeks puppies should have other items of medical care. Among these are a good physical exam, the establishment of an antiparasite program (both external and internal) and the maintenance of a good health record, usually started by the person who owns the mother dog.

The first visit many puppies make to the veterinarian, however, is made before they are three days old. This visit is to get their tails docked and/or their dew claws clipped. By getting this done early in their lives, it reduces discomfort to a minimum, controls hemorrhage and eliminates the need for sutures, allowing the spot to heal almost without scar. (It also will not scar your pocket book, as it would if you waited until the bone had hardened and full-scale amputation had to be resorted to.)

The puppy's next visit (or, if it is a breed whose tail is not docked, or dew claws are left on, its first visit) to the veterinarian is usually the one where the puppy receives its first vaccinations. At that time the puppy should also be checked for internal parasites, such as hookworms or roundworms, and the pup should be given a complete physical examination.

A complete physical exam will reveal such congenital problems as anal stenosis, patent ductus arteriosis, persistent right aortic arch, hydrocephalus, inguinal and umbilical hernias and other, less common, defects. Some of these problems, if severe, can be recognized by anyone. Others, often more subtle in nature, require a veterinarian to diagnose.

Any internal parasites discovered during these early visits should be properly treated. Over-the-counter worm remedies are often ineffective for this worm treatment. Medication administered by a veterinarian is specifically designed to kill the particular worm in question, and, under veterinary supervision, can be given at the highest doses necessary to achieve maximum worm kill.

The second visit to the veterinarian usually occurs about 14 to 21 days following the first and is for second vaccinations and second worm treatment, if needed. This visit is usually made by the new owner of the puppy, since most people who breed dogs like to place their puppies with their new owners as soon after weaning as possible.

If you are selling puppies, you should always tell your buyer the exact date the puppy was born, weaned, received its initial DHL-P or Parvo vaccinations and, if it had worms, when and for what worms it was treated.

If you are a new puppy buyer, you should insist that the individual from whom you purchase the puppy gives you the *exact* date the puppy was born, weaned, received its distemper and Parvo vaccinations and, if treated for worms, what those worms were.

These facts will become the first information to be put in your puppy's health record. In addition to vaccinations and worming dates, your puppy's health record should also contain a monthly weight until the puppy is 12 months old, any dietary changes made and, of course, any accidental injuries, illnesses, etc.

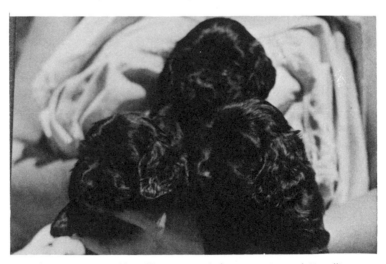

The importance of handling can never be overestimated. Handling teaches puppies to trust people and rely on them for many needs.

126

6

New Home Environment: Weeks Seven to Twelve

W E CALL THIS PERIOD the Age of Transition II because puppies usually go into their new homes somewhere between the age of seven and 12 weeks of age. Most people acquire puppies when the puppy is about eight weeks old. Breeders of small and toy-sized breeds frequently hold them until the puppies are between 12 and 16 weeks of age simply because the puppies are so small and the breeders are concerned for their safety and welfare. They feel their particular breeds aren't as mature at eight weeks of age as the mid- or large-sized breeds.

Providing the puppy gets plenty of animal and human socialization and lots of new experiences in the outside world between the age of seven and 16 weeks of age, the puppy will be capable of developing to its fullest potential later on. I know a few breeders who are so conscientious that they work with their puppies every day until they go into new homes. I've also known some who do nothing except the barest essentials of physical care and when those puppies grow up, they show the scars of the deprivation for life.

Regardless of breed, there will be no better time in the puppy's life for it to make the adjustment from birth environment to new home. So many things are happening inside that little furry body— the brain, nervous system and muscles are all making new behaviors possible. Body changes are occurring daily and the puppy's needs

Great Pyrenees: Giant breeds have special needs and anyone contemplating acquiring a giant puppy should be familiar with those needs in advance. —*Percy T. Jones*

German Shepherd siblings will soon outgrow the bushel basket they're posed in. Dogs of breeds with naturally erect ears sometimes need help in getting the ears to stand. In most cases, ears will usually come up by themselves.

become more complex almost by the hour. Most of all, the degree of attraction to humans that the puppy feels between seven and nine weeks will stay with him for life. This is the stage in the puppy's life when it is best suited to bond with new people and a new home. In short, the puppy is ready.

During the early stage of this period, the puppy begins to indicate an interest in and the desire for care and attention by licking humans as well as its dam. Most breeds develop the tail-wagging behavior that tells us the puppy is happy or pleased about something. It no longer needs to sleep in a pile with its littermates and begins to sleep apart from them. The dam's milk begins to dry up and the puppy begins to eat independently. In other words, the puppy becomes totally aware of its environment and begins to react to it. Finally, it learns that it can survive without its mother and is ready to take its place in a new home.

A Fear Period

There is, however, a short period when one must be extremely cautious about changing the puppy's environment. That is the fear period at age eight weeks. Unlike the brief one at five weeks of age when the startle response was activating, this one can last longer, be more intense and have more lasting effects on the final outcome of the puppy's development.

While the cause of the fifth week fear period was muscle and neurological development, the cause of the eighth week fear period is more complex. The dam initiates the onset of this second fear period when she begins, gently at first, threatening the puppies as they nurse. This behavior serves two purposes. It signals the beginning of the end of the dam providing total nourishment for the puppy. Further, it designates the beginning of allelomimetic behavior, or group activities.

Since dogs are a social animal and can only survive in the wild by forming packs and hunting together, puppies must learn how to function in group activities while they are with their littermates. They must learn about fear and how to use the group to overcome their adversaries.

By eight weeks, the memory portion of the brain is fully mature and puppies do not forget. Consequently, if they're frightened or threatened by a person or experience at the onset of this maturation period, they will remember it and avoid it.

In some puppies, this period is very obvious to the owner. One day, for example, the puppy will accept the vacuum cleaner as a routine part of the household. Then suddenly, at about 55 to 58 days of age, the puppy will dash from the room when the vacuum is brought out of the closet. The wise owner will ignore this behavior and act nonchalantly and proceed with his or her cleaning. Within a day or two, the puppy will once again accept the vacuum. If, however, the owner forces the puppy to accept it, it may result in permanent fear of the vacuum.

Fear, which is a natural emotional response to an outside stimuli, manifests itself in different ways in different dogs. Some breeds, for example, experience the fear period longer than others. Some breeds arrive at the period at $7\frac{1}{2}$ weeks while others don't experience it until almost nine weeks. Some dogs need more human support than others and some pass through this stage so subtly the owner never notices it. All dogs, however, need positive experiences to modify their fear responses at this impressionable age.

Therefore, transferring a puppy to a new environment during this critical fear period could produce permanent damage to its emotional stability. For this reason and many others which we will discuss in future pages, the period from seven to 12 weeks is the ideal age to place a puppy in its new home with the exception of the few days just prior to and following its eighth week.

Feeding the New Puppy

Formulating the correct diet for the weanling puppy is one of the most important steps in starting a dog's life. The only source of nourishment a rapidly growing puppy receives comes exclusively from what its owner puts down for it to eat. The puppy's health and growth will be a reflection of how well the feeding job is done.

The growing puppy should be weighed weekly for the first six months of its life. The weekly growth rate, from weaning to six months, should be constant that it forms a straight line when plotted on a graph (see Figures 6.1 and 6.2).

Puppies obtained after weaning already have a feeding program. Make every effort to find out everything you can about that feeding program from the old owner. Determine which food was being used, feeding times and amounts fed so you can duplicate them for at least a few days until the pup has become accustomed to its new surroundings. Continue to feed the rapidly growing puppy the same

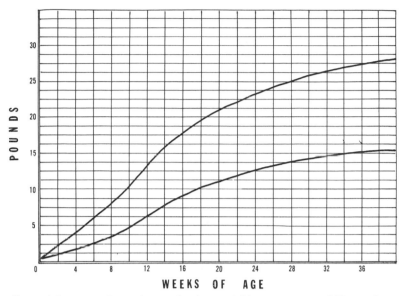

Figure 6.1. A normal growth curve for dogs weighing an average of 20 pounds as an adult.

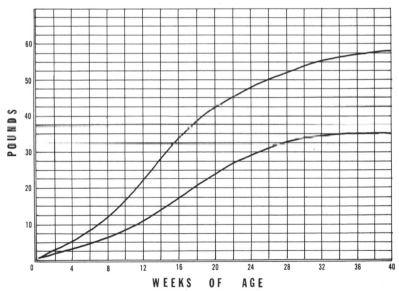

Figure 6.2. A normal growth curve for dogs weighing an average of 50 pounds as an adult.

food that was used to wean it, but gradually add additional foods to train the puppy's inexperienced digestive system.

Do not be afraid to change the old routine, however. Never be misled into feeding a new puppy what and how its previous owner fed it just because you feel that owner is an experienced dog feeder. Some of the most false and potentially harmful information about dog feeding I ever heard was perpetuated by experienced dog owners.

For the first six to eight months of its life, the puppy will be both growing, and using nutrients and energy, at a fantastic rate. In fact, the rapidly growing puppy needs twice as much energy and nutrients per pound of body weight as an adult dog. The energy and nutrients must be in a form that is digestible by the puppy's inexperienced digestive tract.

Canned and soft-moist foods will, as a group, contain ingredients of higher digestibility than dry foods. There are exceptions of course, and a few dry foods containing easily digestible nutrients are much better for feeding rapidly growing puppies than numerous canned foods containing poorly digestible nutrients.

To determine the quantity of food to start feeding any rapidly growing puppy, determine the number of calories per pound of body weight your puppy should be fed for its age (see Table 6.1). Divide the number of calories contained in a pound of the food you are feeding into the number of calories your puppy needs every day to find out what quantity of food (in pounds) you should offer initially.

If the puppy cleans up every bit offered for three days in a row, add five percent more food to the daily feeding. If it continues to eat everything it is offered for three more days, add five percent more food again. Continue to add food at this rate until the puppy leaves a tiny bit at each meal. It is possible, with a rapidly growing puppy, that you may never reach a point at which it will leave any food until it is practically grown. There is no need to worry about this unless the puppy fails to gain the same amount of weight each week as it did the week before.

Pups from six weeks to four months of age should be fed four times daily; from four months to 12 months, three times daily; and after 12 months, twice daily.

Between ten and 12 months of age (12 and 14 months in large breeds), the rate at which a puppy grows begins to slow down. At the same time the dog's food consumption also begins to drop noticeably. This is a normal occurrence, brought about by the reduction in the dog's need for the extra nutrients and energy required during rapid growth. Novices sometimes mistake this reduction in food consumption as an indication of illness. Alert, experienced dog feeders know that when maturity brings about this reduction in food intake, it is time to stop feeding puppy foods and start feeding adult maintenance diets.

Table 6.1

Daily Caloric Needs of Puppies

Body weight in pounds

Weeks	1	2	3	4	5	10	15	20	25	30	40	50	60	70
5	100	200	300	400	500	1000	1500							
6	90	180	270	360	450	900	1350							
7	80	160	240	320	400	800	1200							
8	75	150	225	300	375	750	1125	1500						
9	70	140	210	280	350	700	1050	1400						
10		130	195	260	325	650	975	1300	1625					
11			180	240	300	600	900	1200	1500					
12				224	280	560	840	1128	1400	1680				
13				208	260	520	780	1040	1300	1560				
14					240	480	720	960	1200	1440	1920			
15						450	675	900	1125	1350	1800			
16						420	630	840	1050	1260	1680	2100		
17							585	780	975	1170	1560	1950		
18								720	900	1080	1440	1800	2160	
19									825	990	1320	1650	1980	
20										900	1280	1500	1800	2100

To determine the number of calories needed by a particular puppy, find the dog's weight in the top row of figures and move downward until you come to the column corresponding to the dog's age in the left-hand row of figures. The figure in that square caused by the intersection of the two columns is the number of calories that puppy should eat during a 24-hour period.

Caring for the Puppy

What kind of care is involved with a new puppy? This is probably the question most frequently asked by people who are about to acquire a new puppy. In addition to Dr. Collins' advice on feeding, there are a few basic guidelines that can be applied to make the job easy and enjoyable.

1. *Hold a family conference before you bring the puppy home.* Establish the rules of conduct that you will expect the puppy to live by for its entire life. For example, if you won't want the dog to jump on people when it weighs 125 pounds, pledge to teach it not to jump right from the start. How about furniture? Will it be allowed on the sofa? If the answer is no, don't let it get started. Keep it on the floor. Who will feed and exercise the puppy and where will you expect it to eliminate? Who will be responsible for its grooming and veterinary care? Who will teach it how to be a polite pet and discipline it?

Once these questions are answered, the process of rearing the puppy can proceed smoothly, and become a rewarding experience for everyone—including the dog. Most dogs who start out life with sound temperaments and go astray usually do so because the humans in their lives are not consistently the leaders.

2. *Have all the necessary equipment ready before you get the puppy.* You will need food and water bowls, a simple buckle collar and lead, a brush, a crate plus the food products used by the breeder to keep the puppy's diet identical to the diet it was on in its first home. As for a crate, we've discussed that subject in detail in Chapter 5. They can be purchased from pet stores and pet product outlets and wholesalers.

3. *Plan on bringing the puppy home when someone is going to be available to get it off to a good start in its new home.* It will prove disastrous to pick up a puppy on Sunday night when the entire family goes off to work on Monday morning, leaving the puppy alone in a crate all day.

A puppy needs to play and exercise and eat regularly while growing. Obtaining a puppy is a big responsibility and should never be taken lightly. Frequently, busy families plan on getting a puppy during summer vacation when they have more time and family members available to raise the new addition. If the puppy is going into a home where everyone in the household works and there will be no extended periods of time to spend with it, at least it can be brought home on a Friday night so the owners will have the entire weekend to spend acclimating the puppy to its new home. In cases such as this, a neighbor or relative can be called in during the daytime when the family is away to feed and exercise the puppy. Eight or nine hours is just too long a period of time to leave a young puppy in a crate alone.

4. *Teach young, children how to interact with the puppy.* Young children and growing puppies are so similar in the ways they behave that they both need supervision and lessons in cohabitating. Pulling on the puppy's ears, tail or legs and poking fingers into its mouth and eyes will only serve to make the puppy hate children.

The way they play together is another important behavior that must be clearly defined and learned. Playing with pull-toys and tug-of-war is out. Both behaviors teach the puppy how effective its jaws and teeth can be. Remember, the puppy is going through the play fighting stage of development in preparation for serious fighting *and winning* as an adult! If it never learns to pull on little children's clothes, shoes, arms and legs, it will not be in the habit of doing it when grown.

Parents must take the time to teach children how to play gently with the puppy in nonthreatening activities, and teach the puppy how to enjoy the children while exercising self-control. Time spent now teaching puppies and children to interact properly with each other is one of the best investments a person can make in developing a meaningful relationship between dog and children later on.

Children must learn not to tease the puppy, particularly at feeding time. The puppy should be fed, and if the children want to watch the puppy eat they should be made to sit quietly until the dog is finished. The dog, on the other hand, should be allowed to eat its meals without being threatened or annoyed. However, it is not unreasonable to expect the puppy to allow its food bowl to be removed for a short period of time (10 to 15 seconds) and then replaced. Have the puppy learn that a human may, from time to time, take away the food bowl and replace it and that he must not growl or bite. It will be too late to teach this behavior to an adult.

5. *Recognize that young puppies need constant supervision.* As stated in detail in Chapter 5, puppies left alone to their own devices will almost certainly get into trouble, one way or the other— probably both! They may eliminate indoors and destroy objects belonging to the people in the household. Both are undesirable and

The love passing between Blair, the little girl, and the Labrador Retriever puppy, and David, the little boy, and the Cocker Spaniel puppy is very obvious. Note that in each case an adult is nearby to supervise the interaction between small child and puppy.

—*Charlotte Schwartz*

will undermine the healthy, happy relationship between puppy and owners. Crate the puppy when you can't be with it and supervise it when you are. Puppyhood doesn't last forever—bad habits do.

6. *Finally, enjoy raising the puppy and relax.* One of the biggest problems with humans is that they get disturbed about too many details and often lose their perspectives. Remember why you got the puppy, vow to enjoy it as you train just as you would enjoy raising a child and you'll end up with a wonderful companion who will be your friend for many years to come.

Localization

Localization—the process whereby a puppy becomes attached to a specific place—begins during weeks six and seven and continues for several more weeks. Here is another important reason why puppies should go to their new home during the Human Socialization Period.

The attachment to a specific place is, it seems, stronger in some breeds than others. Many breeders of the working, herding and terrier breeds have told me how devoted to specific places their breeds become. Hounds and sporting dogs, however, seem to be the happy-go-lucky types who love everyone and every place. Running and enjoying life in general, they just don't get overly attached to any one particular locale. The reason probably has something to do with the fact that they are bred to hunt, an activity that can take them many miles over a period of hours.

Whatever the breed or the reason for a strong predisposition to localization, it must be recognized by breeders and puppy owners alike. The puppy who will be most likely to be affected by it should be settled in its permanent home during this period of environmental attachment.

Territoriality and Order of Dominance

Once the puppy gets settled in its new home, it will begin to sort out the people and places within that environment and its own relationship to them. In other words, the puppy begins to establish its own territory and preference for certain pack members.

All puppies are born pushy, some more than others. The species would not have survived without that innate drive to stay on top and procreate its own kind. However, for a pack to flourish there can be only one leader. So through play fighting and interacting with its littermates in group activities, the puppy learns that one individual is dominant and all others fall somewhere beneath the leader. When a puppy transfers from the original pack of its dam and littermates to a human pack in the new owner's home, it tries again to become the leader.

The new owner must provide a specific territory for the puppy and teach it that this is, in fact, its domain. The puppy must learn where it belongs, who are its pack members and who is the leader. All this can be accomplished peacefully if done correctly.

In Chapter 5 we discussed crate training, which spells out quite clearly the dog's sleeping area and resting place. Always exercising the puppy in one spot will teach the location of the elimination area. The puppy should be taken to a wide variety of places as part of its socialization, and it should be encouraged to make friends with humans wherever it goes. The owner must refrain from acting in an overly solicitous and protective manner or the puppy will grow up to be shy and afraid.

To help the puppy learn right from the beginning that all the humans in its pack are dominant but that it does have a position within the pack, the puppy should be given the Dominance Down. Complete directions are given in Chapter 5.

Ideally, the human leader of the family should do the Dominance Down first. Once he or she establishes a leadership role over the puppy—and he or she will know because the puppy will respond more freely to this person and act as if especially fond of the leader—then all other family members should establish their position above the puppy. When the hierarchy of the household has been established, all the members, humans and puppy alike, will be comfortable with the pack and begin to function effectively as a viable unit.

Puppy Proofing Your Home

For everyone's protection and happiness, the following guidelines are offered:

- Keep toxic and harmful objects out of puppy's reach. Medicines, cigarettes, nail polish, cleaning fluids, antifreeze, bug repellents, garbage and trash, soaps and detergents, shrubs and houseplants are all dangerous, some are poisonous.

138

- Make sure the puppy cannot chew on electric wiring of any kind.
- Close access to areas you do not want the puppy in. Open stairways and closet doors invite puppies to investigate, which can lead to its getting hurt or in trouble.
- Shoes, socks and clothes left laying on the floor present open invitations to chew.
- Items placed on low coffee tables can easily be reached and destroyed by curious puppies.
- Puppies love to chew newspapers, magazines and books. Keep them up high until the puppy grows older.
- Never leave a puppy unsupervised, even for a few minutes. Major accidents happen when you turn your back "for just a minute."
- Never give a puppy the freedom to wander alone through a house or it may mistake rooms for elimination areas.

Early Schooling

Even though the puppy is very young and only a fraction the size of what it will be at maturity, it can and should begin to learn some basic behaviors of good conduct. Remember, although its little body may be clumsy and not very strong at this age, its brain is fully matured. So teaching a few simple behaviors will get the puppy off to the right start before it has time to establish some bad habits.

Lead Training

Lead training is perhaps the most important early lesson. It allows the owner to control the puppy and assures that the puppy will always be safe when outdoors. To start, the puppy should be given a lightweight buckle collar to wear for a day or so. At first, the puppy will probably scratch at it many times in an effort to get it off his neck. When you see him scratching, simply divert his attention to a toy and he'll soon forget about it.

Once accustomed to the collar, snap the lead onto it and let the puppy drag the lead around the room for a few minutes. Don't pick up the lead at this time. Just give the puppy a chance to feel the weight of the lead on the collar.

The next day, carry the puppy outdoors, away from the elimination area, and set him on the ground about 20 feet from the

This young lad has already begun training his dog, a yellow Labrador Retriever, in an obedience class. The two will grow and learn together, developing a bond between them that will last a lifetime.
—*Charlotte Schwartz*

140

door. Pick up the end of the lead and slowly walk toward the door. The puppy is now familiar with his home and will be eager to return to familiar surroundings. If he hurries ahead of you, let him lead the way with you holding the end of the lead.

Over the next few days graduate the distance the puppy walks so he becomes used to walking within the confines of the length of the lead. When he acts confident with the pressure of the lead, turn and walk a short distance away from the door and then turn around again and let him lead you back to the house.

Remember, never pull or snap the collar or lead against the puppy's neck. Severe damage can result from heavy-handed lead training. When he gets a little older, you can get him into a formal class and teach him many things, including how to walk by your side. But, for now, we want the puppy to learn that being on a collar and lead is an exciting, wonderful activity.

If done correctly, the average puppy will learn to walk on a lead within a few days. And then you and the puppy can begin to investigate a new world together.

Come

"Come!" can be the most exciting word a puppy can ever learn if it's taught properly. Taught incorrectly it can make your puppy want to run away. The choice is in the hands of the owner.

To teach a little puppy to come when called, simply drop down to your knees, alternately open your arms wide and clap your hands as you call excitedly "Puppy, come!" Keep your voice happy and excited and keep calling. Saying it once may get the puppy's attention, but it will take a lot more "Come on, puppy. That's a good boy!" to get him running to you.

When the puppy arrives let him know you think he's the best little critter in the whole world and coming to you was the most marvelous thing he's ever done. Tell him he's a super puppy and really love him up. Celebrate with him and he'll never forget the wonderful reception he received when he came to you.

Speaking sternly, barking out commands like a Marine sergeant or spanking the puppy because he didn't come or came too slowly will only serve to teach the puppy not to come at all next time. You've got to make it happen for the puppy. You've got to show him that coming to you always produces positive experiences. And you must never let him see you become frustrated or angry.

If you spend the time and exert the energy to keep the atmosphere alive with excitement while the puppy is young and vulnerable, you'll produce an adult that will always come when called. Remember, most occasions when a person wants a dog to come to them is when there is some other stimuli in the environment—a cat, a wandering dog, a stranger. If you teach your puppy to come quickly every time you call, he'll come despite the distraction when he's an adult.

Sit

Teaching a puppy to sit on command is very easy. Place two or three fingers in the collar at the top of the neck with your fingertips facing toward his tail. Run your other hand down his spine, over his tail to his hock joint (knees). As you pull up on the collar and tuck his rear end under him, say "Sit."

Once sitting, tell him how wonderful he is. Go crazy. Celebrate your joy with him. Again, let him think he's a genius. Do this several times a day for a week and you'll find him sitting automatically whenever you say "Sit." You can wean off the physical help with your hands as soon as you see him begin to respond to the word command. Always praise him when he obeys.

A note of caution: Never slap the puppy's rear end, never tell him more than once and never lose your temper. All these things just serve to convince the puppy that he doesn't like sitting and, what's worse, that he doesn't like learning from you because you hurt or nag him.

Down

Down is another very useful behavior to teach your puppy and can be done amazingly well with the use of food. What you're doing here is conditioning the dog to the sound of the word "down" and the downward motion of your hand. If done correctly, you can wean off the food and the dog will always drop to the floor whenever told to "Down." Furthermore, he'll do it willingly because he wasn't forced and has made the association that "down" signals the onset of a positive experience for him.

To teach the down, get on your knees and have the puppy sit next to your left side. Place your left hand ever-so-lightly over his shoulders just below the base of his neck. This hand will not push the puppy to the floor, but will, instead, simply guide him down alongside of you.

With a tasty morsel of chicken or cheese or some other nutritious food in your right hand show the puppy the treat. Place the treat right in front of his nose as he sits next to you. You can let him lick it, but don't let him eat it just yet. Using your voice psyche him up so that he really wants that treat.

Now slowly lower your right hand from in front of his nose down to his feet and then straight out in front of him making an imaginary "L." As you make the "L" and the puppy's nose follows the treat down and out in front, say "Down" softly. The puppy will drop to the floor as he reaches for the treat in your hand when it gets out in front of him. The moment his elbows touch the floor release the food and, using your left hand, stroke him gently while you tell him he's a good boy. Let him stay in the down position as he eats the treat, and keep telling him how wonderful he is.

A few words of warning: Should the puppy stand up at any time while you're in the process of making the "L," resit him and begin again. This time, use your left forearm placed along his spine to prevent him from popping up as his head follows the treat down toward his feet. Your left hand should remain over his shoulders as before.

Teaching the down with food can best be accomplished just prior to feeding time when the puppy is hungry. A few downs several times a day will have him responding to the word and the hand signal from his nose area down to the floor in front of him within a week or two.

Some puppies willingly drop to the floor on the command "Down," but they pop right back up again as soon as they've eaten the treat. It seems they quickly figure out that if they sit up, you'll give them another treat to drop again so it becomes an annoying routine: you say "Down," the puppy drops, you give the treat, then he pops up, you produce another treat to get the next down. Pretty soon, you feel like the puppy is training you!

To prevent that from happening, keep the puppy in the down position for a few seconds until you give him a release word such as "OK!" If he does sit up before you release him, simply take his front feet and gently slide them forward so that he drops into the down position again and tell him to "Wait." Count to five, and then release him with "OK, good boy!" Do not produce another treat when he gets up before he's released otherwise he'll keep sitting up as soon as he's eaten. One treat for one command and then a release from you with praise. The next treat will come only when you give a new "Down" command at a later time.

In Chapter 8 we will discuss formal training—what it is, what it shouldn't be, where to find a quality training program and how to get started. But for now lead training, come, sit and down get you the control you must have to build a bond together and develop a working relationship. In Chapter 8 we also discuss specialized training, which offers a lifetime of fun and activities for you and your dog.

Keeping Your Puppy Well Groomed

Keeping your puppy looking its best is really quite easy if attended to regularly. The following tips will aid in this owner's task:

- Keep the puppy's nails cut. Long nails cause discomfort and can change the way a puppy walks by forcing it to put too much weight on the back part of the foot.
- Keep the puppy's ears clean. Wipe out the ears with a piece of cotton or tissue dipped in 3 percent alcohol, warm water or baby oil.
- With long-coated puppies, be sure the hair around the anus does not collect feces. If necessary, keep the hair trimmed short to facilitate cleanliness and ease of maintenance.
- Brush the puppy at least three times a week. Short-coated dogs should be brushed with a soft bristle brush. Long-coated breeds should be brushed with a hard bristle or wire bristle brush (sometimes called a "slicker brush").
- In winter be sure snow does not collect between the pads of the feet and cause sores. Salt used to melt snow can burn the skin between the pads. Each time the puppy goes outdoors in snowy weather, towel dry its feet when the puppy comes indoors.
- Look at the puppy's teeth daily and check for loose teeth, swollen gums, foreign objects caught between teeth and a build-up of tartar. Your veterinarian can clean the puppy's teeth when necessary, but preventative care goes a long way toward making those procedures infrequent. If you can, brush the puppy's teeth daily with a regular tooth brush and

plain water. It really helps and, if started early, the puppy will not object at all.

- Dried matter that collects in the corner of the eyes should be removed daily. If you notice an unusual discharge from the eyes, see your veterinarian.
- Breeds that require professional grooming, clipping, plucking and trimming should be groomed professionally. It is possible for the pet owner to learn to groom his or her own dog, but it takes time, practice and lots of training from a professional to do it correctly.
- Whenever you're grooming your puppy, it should be placed above the floor on a nonslip table or raised surface. Teach the puppy from the beginning that being on a table means it's grooming time and squirming and playing are out of order. When you're finished, put the puppy down on the floor and give a special treat such as a biscuit. You'll be amazed to see how quickly the little fellow learns that grooming time is a special time that always ends with a treat.

Play

Puppies aren't born knowing how to play. They learn first with their littermates, trying out a variety of behaviors and observing the reactions. Things that bring them pleasure, they retain. Things that bring pain or unhappiness, they abandon.

By the time they get into their new homes they've begun to demonstrate their desire to play with a group (their littermates), to play fight and spar (in preparation for adult hunting, killing and territorial defense), and to interact with humans when it results in pleasure.

From this point on, the toys and types of play involving the puppy will have a direct result on the dog when an adult. Toy and play sessions are almost as important as proper diet and control training.

Hard rubber toys, balls, natural processed bones, old socks tied into knots, empty plastic milk cartons and squeaky toys (providing they don't destroy them and eat the squeakers!) are safe toys for puppies. If the puppy chews up a toy it should be discarded before the dog has an opportunity to eat it because bits and pieces of plastic, rubber, rags, etc. can block the intestine and cause suffering and even death.

How you play with the puppy and its toys is extremely important. As we stated in Chapter 5, tug-of-war and games that incite the puppy's bite reflexes should never be encouraged. Games of fetch, hide and seek and lazy walks that offer plenty of opportunity to investigate the environment are ideal for dogs of all ages. Taking the four basic control exercises and making them games can be fun and profitable for puppy and owner. There is no reason why schooling and game time can't intermingle. Both are necessary to develop the puppy into the perfect adult pet. And adult dogs, when trained properly, love to work for and with their owners. They see it as a major activity in their lives. In Chapter 9 we'll give you some ideas to take games into the realm of useful jobs for the adult dog's sense of fulfillment.

As pointed out earlier, puppies in this period love to carry objects. Consequently, this is an ideal time to teach retrieving, or fetch. To get the puppy to run out, pick up an object and return it to you, the puppy must be wearing his collar and lead.

First show the puppy one of his favorite toys, one that he hasn't seen for a day or two because you deliberately put it out of sight for awhile. Wiggle it in front of him but just beyond his reach. Make him want to reach for it and grab it. Then toss it out in front of the puppy about six to eight feet away. As he lurches for it, go with him, never allowing the lead to snap taut, which would act as a correction for chasing it. When you get to the toy, reach down and wiggle it again and when the puppy shows interest in it or grabs it let him take it in his mouth. As he does say, "Fetch, good fetch!"

Next, begin to back up having the puppy follow you with the toy in his mouth. Keep your hands low in front of his face and clap them excitedly to show him where you want him to be. When you get back to the spot you started from, take the toy out of his mouth and say "Out." Then go into the happy-happy routine and tell him he's wonderful.

Do this several times a day until the puppy begins to look forward to his new fetch game. Always make it fun for him and always stop before he tires of it. If you've done it three times and he still wants one more chance, quit. He'll be left with the memory of wanting one more opportunity to chase, capture and retrieve for you.

As the puppy becomes proficient at the retrieve, put him on a 20-foot line and throw the toy further. Also, as he begins to

One way puppies demonstrate their intelligence is by problem solving. Ultimately this Cocker puppy will get the ball off the table. At this point he's determining how he will do it.

—*Percy T. Jones*

147

anticipate the chase and runs out ahead of you, stop going with him. Let him go out and retrieve the toy by himself and carry it back to you. Shortly, you'll find he'll be ready to try retrieving other objects for longer distances, knowing there's a celebration waiting when he brings it back.

Never allow a dog to catch and retrieve a ball that might lodge in his throat because it is too small for his mouth. Plain white tennis balls are fine for little puppies and medium-sized adults, but big dogs need big balls. Finally, when the puppy gets good at retrieving try something new.

As he's running toward you with his prize in his mouth, turn and walk away from him so that he'll arrive at your side instead of in front of you. As he begins to accept this new position of yours, try getting him to carry it alongside as you walk together. He'll love carrying his toys to the yard for a play session and he'll be learning how to carry other objects when he gets older.

A puppy needs a few short play sessions every day. Two five-minute sessions are adequate for the average puppy up to 12 weeks of age. After that you can lengthen one session or add another short one until, as an adult, the dog can look forward to a 20- to 30-minute daily play session. These sessions should always be in areas that provide total security for the dog. If, for example, a puppy runs out to fetch a ball and discovers a rabbit in the grass he may take off after the rabbit and run across the road or into someone else's yard. If you cannot provide a fenced area for play, keep him on a long line and he'll still get plenty of exercise and enjoyment out of it.

Playing with other animals is fine, providing there is proper supervision. However, allowing a large breed to play roughly with a toy breed or other pet can be dangerous or fatal to the small partner. Many years ago, I had a client who had a lovely Doberman Pinscher who, when he matured, played toss and fetch with a tiny Yorkshire Terrier and killed it. Needless to say the owner was devastated and never forgave the Doberman when, in fact, it wasn't the big dog's fault. He'd been playing roughly with the little one all his life and nobody had ever stopped him. Then one day he got too rough and it was all over.

7

The Juvenile Period: Twelve Weeks to Six Months

GROWING UP IS both exciting and stressful to all animals, your puppy included. How the puppy progresses through this difficult, yet delightful stage depends in great part on you.

Understanding what goes on in a puppy's head and why it acts the way it does during the Juvenile Period is possible only when we understand all the changes occurring to the puppy during this time. Some are very subtle, some obvious, all take the puppy one step closer to maturity.

By approximately 12 to 13 weeks of age, all the puppy's sense organs are developed. The puppy can hear, see, taste, smell and feel to the fullest extent. Training at a later stage in life can polish those senses to a fine point, but it will not increase their development. For example, olfactory training can sharpen the dog's awareness of what it smells and teach the dog to discriminate between different scents, but such training cannot increase the olfactory capabilities beyond what they were at 13 weeks of age.

The brain, which was completely developed by five to six weeks, begins to control the puppy's emotions and direct its body to react to its perception of the environment. Emotional maturation begins somewhere between 13 and 16 weeks of age and will continue for some time. The level of maturity that a dog eventually reaches is dependent upon heredity, social relationships and the personality of the individual. Furthermore, we must remember that behavior is not fixed. Genetics and developmental processes will cause constant changes throughout a dog's lifetime.

Motor skills continue to develop and gain strength but they will not be completely developed until the dog is much older. Complete physical development is usually achieved by two years of age for most dogs. However, some large and heavily coated breeds may not be fully mature until they are three or more.

Agonistic behavior, fighting usually involving domination/subordination patterns, begins at about seven weeks of age and is highly developed by the time the puppy is 15 weeks old. When a puppy has the opportunity to live with its littermates until the seventh or eighth week, it learns a great deal about dominant/submissive relationships. When the puppy moves into its new home, it has already had an important lesson in how to get along with other dogs. Consequently, the puppy at 15 weeks and beyond has a better chance of interacting peacefully with other dogs as it matures if it's been with its littermates up to at least seven weeks of age.

Up to 15 or 16 weeks of age, the puppy is generally very friendly to all people, family and strangers alike. After this period the puppy's capacity to socialize declines. If it has experienced pleasure during the first 15 weeks of life, it will probably enjoy people forever. If it hasn't, it may never learn to like them. From this point on the puppy's tolerance of strangers will also depend, in part, on its breed.

Teething

A puppy's permanent teeth begin to emerge at 16 weeks of age. This can be a painful process for the puppy and cause it to do a lot of chewing. Providing the puppy with soft chew toys, an old sock with some ice cubes tied in the toe and soft, palatable food can help. At this time, owners often find baby teeth around the house where they fall out of the puppy's mouth as it chews on a toy.

When the puppy reaches approximately eight months of age, it will go through another teething period. At this time, the molars will be breaking through the gums and the puppy will probably enter into a period of intensive chewing and gnawing.

Often, the owner is caught off guard when this happens and loses valuable furniture and other possessions. The scenario goes

150

Even for a big, strapping youngster like this 4½-month-old Irish Wolfhound, this chain choke collar is too large. Puppies outgrow their collars rapidly, so should wear inexpensive ones until their growing is complete. Some regard chain chokes unsafe for puppies.

Mouthing anything and everything is perfectly normal for developing puppies. Owners must be watchful against the possibility of puppies getting hold of any potentially dangerous materials. —*Thomas Melvin Studios*

something like this: The puppy grows large, responds well to training and presents no behavior problems in the home. The owner, lulled by a false sense of security, no longer crates the dog when he goes away thinking that, since the puppy hasn't chewed up anything in several months, it's probably past the chewing stage. However, the molars begin to hurt the gums at the back of the mouth and the owner isn't aware of the emerging teeth. The owner goes away, leaving the dog free to roam the house. Puppy's gums hurt so he begins gnawing on the leg of a table or the arm of a chair. By the time the owner arrives home, the damage has been done and the owner can't understand why the puppy regressed.

The fact of the matter is that the puppy didn't regress—it simply satisfied a need to chew. Only this time, the chewing urge was more intense and only large pieces of furniture satisfied the need. Punishing the dog at this point would be useless and even counterproductive to training it to stay alone in the future.

The best prevention for this situation is to expect it. Don't think the dog is ready to be given the freedom of the house just because it hasn't chewed things recently. Wait until you're sure that all teeth are in and that the puppy is truly past the chewing stage. If you're not sure, have your veterinarian check the puppy's mouth at about seven months of age to determine the status of the emerging molars. The cost of a visit to your veterinarian is far less than the price of a new sofa or chair!

Another Fear Period

As the weeks turn into months, the puppy enters a third fear period, which occurs between the fourth and seventh month. Like the one before it, it may last an hour, a day or a week. With some puppies, the owner may never even notice it.

Owner reaction to this fear period should be identical to the previous one. Ignore it. Don't make an issue out of the puppy being afraid of new or even some old situations. This fear period will pass quite naturally.

Finally, there may come a time when the puppy defies the owner. In large breeds this can happen at eight or 18 months. With smaller breeds it is usually closer to the eighth month. The dog is testing again and if you can calmly, but firmly, insist that it obey and comply with your wishes the phase will pass without incident.

Being permissive is lethal to the relationship. It only serves to let the puppy know that you really don't think you're the leader. It opens the door for the puppy to step into the role of leadership and, when this happens, the entire hierarchy will tumble. Being openly aggressive may encourage the puppy to react with aggressive violence. Either way, the owner's ability to handle a crisis situation is on the line. Calm firmness in the face of a challenge is the only way to see it through without permanent damage resulting.

My own German Shepherd Dog, Morgan, tested me once when he was eight months old and again when he was 17 months. Both times, I took a deep breath, regrouped my thoughts, gently, but firmly, insisted he obey and he did. Morgan is now three years old and my most devoted companion. He also understands that I love him dearly but will not tolerate disobedience and will never step down as pack leader.

Sexual Development and Neutering

Sexual development begins at about 16 weeks and continues into adulthood, which is signaled in dogs by leg lifting and ground scratching and in bitches by the onset of estrus (the heat cycle).

Bitches coming into season twice a year can create havoc in a neighborhood. Male dogs wander all over marking shrubs and flowers as well as front porches and automobile tires. They sit on the front lawn at night and howl and make a nuisance of themselves. But most of all, they present a real threat whenever the bitch's owner wants to exercise the female in season. Too often, the whole affair ends up with a litter of unwanted mixed-breed puppies.

What's even worse than all the inconvenience involved with unneutered males and unspayed bitches is the suffering of the dogs themselves. Intact dogs produce hormones that create within them the desire to breed. Unspayed bitches fight off the males in the beginning of estrus and seek them out as ovulation sets in, which is during the middle of the heat cycle. In short, both sexes suffer frustration, which, in turn, creates more problems to their physical health and well-being.

Dogs and bitches that are deliberately kept intact for breeding purposes should be confined and supervised at all times, particularly during times when they could accidentally breed. This, of course, entails secure housing and exercise areas—which are costly to build and frequently forbidden in residential communities. If people are truly dedicated to their breed and want to see only the very best individuals bred to improve the breed, then all others should be neutered.

Most veterinarians will neuter and spay dogs at maturity. It is best to consult your own veterinarian regarding the age at which he or she wishes to do it.

Finally, there are some very good things that happen following neutering. Both males and females are less likely to wander, easier to manage, more lovable and gentle (although they remain good watch dogs for the home) and the multitude of problems associated with breeding can be avoided. Your pet remains your companion, not the neighborhood's.

Living with a puppy during the Juvenile Period is an interesting experience. One day he's a silly puppy, the next he's a very responsible, serious dog. The changes taking place are more inside the puppy than out, and therefore, harder to identify. In the People Socialization Period, the puppy was discovering the world around him. In this one, he's discovering the individual within himself. With knowledgeable, patient owners, both you and he will like what he discovers.

8

You, The New Owner

THERE ARE PROBABLY as many reasons why
people own dogs as there are people in the world. Therefore, it
would be inappropriate to list a dozen or so reasons expecting
everyone to fit into one of those categories. Instead, we can suggest
general areas of interest that motivate people into owning a dog.

The Purpose of Acquiring a Dog

Companionship is a very common reason. In the role of a
full-time companion the dog will live with and accompany the owner
throughout its lifetime. A dog forces us to function. A dog needs
nourishment—you must purchase food for it and prepare and serve
meals regularly. A dog needs to eliminate—you must get outdoors
several times a day, rain or shine, and give the dog an opportunity to
relieve itself. A dog needs daily exercise—another reason to get
outdoors and, in the doing, the owner gets exercise too.

A dog needs training—you must decide on a course of
education, whether it be formal or otherwise, and implement the
dog's schooling. A dog needs attention—since the dog is a social
animal it will not thrive in social isolation. Therefore, you must
recognize your responsibility to provide social interaction with the
dog every day of its life. The more you involve the dog in your
lifestyle, the happier the dog will be. And the happier it is, the more
rewarding will be your relationship with the dog.

Acquiring a dog for a specific purpose, such as field trials, obedience competition or sled dog racing, is another large area of general interest. There are literally dozens of specialized activities that require the involvement of dogs and people together.

Working dogs who function as assistants to mankind are found in law enforcement agencies, on farms and ranches, as guide dogs for the blind and hearing ear dogs for the deaf, and wherever man finds a dog an able assistant to help him accomplish a job. In our crowded technological age, dogs at work aren't as popular as they once were, but the ones who do work with man are considered invaluable helpers.

Perhaps you are one of the millions of people who doesn't want a "total" companion, but simply a dog to act as a friend for the entire family. This is probably the single most popular category of dog ownership. Here again, there is a dog for every family and it can serve to bring the entire family into a closer unit. Recognizing responsibility and designating areas of activity with the dog can afford something for every member of the family from small children to grandparents.

Before acquiring a dog—for whatever reason—it would be helpful to establish your goals for the dog and also consider what you can do in case there ever comes a time when you change those goals. For example, getting a little dog for Grandma is fine providing you plan what will become of the dog if and when Grandma can no longer care for the animal. Don't wait for a crisis to decide. Have a plan of action to take care of just such a situation.

Further, your goal for the dog at the time you acquire it may change because, as the dog develops, you realize the dog can't meet that goal. Will you want to get rid of the dog, or will you have an alternate plan in mind? Buying a dog, for example, to exhibit in conformation classes at dog shows is fine, but if the little fellow doesn't develop the winning physique you expected, will it still be welcome in your home? If not, do you have in mind a course of action to provide the dog with another home? And will the dog be able to make an adjustment to a new environment? Some breeds relocate better than others, and you should consider this before acquiring the puppy.

Lifestyles

Your lifestyle is the key to determining what breed of dog you

156

should have. The availability of time, your living habits, family size and facilities for housing the dog should all be considered.

A busy career person who works long hours during the week and isn't home much on weekends, for example, would make a poor candidate for dog ownership. Dogs can't tolerate the isolation of living alone and seeing the owner for only a few minutes a day.

A family with several small children would do well with one of the happy-type breeds and very poorly with a hyperactive breed that can't tolerate the noise and clamor of growing children.

There are ideal dogs for all types of living quarters and the best person to guide you into the right choice is a breeder who knows your lifestyle and living arrangements. Take the time to investigate which breed of dog is right for you and your lifestyle.

Choosing the Right Breed

Listed in the back of this book is every breed recognized for registration by the American Kennel Club. Every library has books on various breeds of dogs as well as the *AKC Complete Dog Book*. In addition, the American Kennel Club will refer you to breeders in your area when you're ready to start looking. You can write them at 51 Madison Avenue, New York, N.Y. 10010.

Any previous experience you may have with dogs will also serve you well. Perhaps you had a dog as a child and remember what a wonderful companion it was. Or maybe you recall a family dog that had the right personality for your childhood family, but the wrong one for your present family. Talk to people with dogs and find out from them how they evaluate their own dogs. Get to know some dogs yourself. You'll find certain dogs that please you and some that don't. Don't acquire in haste and regret it. Decide before you buy!

Cost and Commitment

Investigate the price of puppies of the breeds that interest you. You may find that one breed is more than you can afford while a similar breed is within your price range.

In addition, consider the cost of maintenance of your chosen breed. How much grooming is involved with the breed and what is the cost? If you acquire a breed that doesn't require professional grooming, but does require lots of brushing, for example, are you prepared to make the commitment to keep it brushed? Brushing an

Time spent in observing young puppies interacting can be very helpful to the prospective buyer, furnishing considerable insights into individual personalities. —*DeoPaul*

Puppies in a well-bred litter should look uniform. An evenness in appearance from one puppy to another is highly desirable and generally points to a well-thought-out breeding program. —*Evelyn M. Shafer*

Old English Sheepdog, for example, is a necessity and a time-consuming activity. But then, a Pomeranian requires brushing, too. Only you can answer these questions. Don't let the seller convince you otherwise.

Immunization, licensing, veterinary visits, medical emergencies, neutering, feeding and general maintenance costs all add up. Be sure you're prepared to assume the responsibility before you make your final decision. Remember, the initial cost of the puppy is only the beginning.

Your Present Skills, Effort and Patience

Your physical skills are another thing you should think about. It would be disastrous, for example, to acquire a puppy that is going to grow up requiring several miles of brisk walking every day if you suffer from arthritis and find walking difficult or impossible. You'd be happier and better off with a dog that needs limited exercise and is happy just playing around the house with you.

On the other hand, if you're a jogger and want a dog to accompany you through the park every morning, get a dog that needs and loves to lope along at a brisk pace for the sheer enjoyment of exercising.

If you have a home at the seashore and love to walk along the beach, one of the water retrieving breeds might be just the breed for you. Certainly, a hunter would look for a hunting breed that is bred to accompany him on his trips.

If teaching tricks is a favorite pastime of yours, one of the small, highly intelligent breeds would suit your needs.

If you are particularly skilled in hiking and camping, a hearty, devoted breed known for its stamina would be right for you. My son, Frank, has a lovely Airedale, Penny, who's been hiking with him up and down the east coast of the United States for years. Penny wears a backpack and carries her own rations. Several times each year they go off together just to be alone in the wilderness and enjoy each other's company.

Choosing the right breed of dog for yourself should include some thought about your own skills, the amount of effort you intend to put into the relationship and the patience you have to work with your canine companion.

Training and Your Attitude About It

How much formal training should a dog have to be a good companion? The answer depends on several factors. First, what is your purpose for owning a dog? What are your goals for the dog once it reaches maturity? How much time and money do you have to invest in its education? Are there any reasons why training the dog would create a hardship to either you or the dog? And finally, what is your attitude regarding formal training? Are you willing to try it?

Let's go back and look at the puppy between the age of eight and 16 weeks of age. The puppy at the beginning of this period is at an optimum stage in its development to begin to learn. By seizing that opportunity to begin its education, both the puppy and the owner will benefit from the results of training for the life of the dog.

Kindergarten Puppy Training (KPT) classes are available in most large cities and mid-sized communities across the country. These classes are for puppies eight to 20 weeks of age and usually consist of one lesson per week for eight weeks. The cost can range from $15 to $75 and is worth every penny.

KPT classes show owners how the puppy learns, what the puppy does and does not understand, how to discipline the puppy, how to use their body as a language to communicate with the puppy and how to teach the puppy a variety of behaviors that will get and keep control. In addition, the owner learns about diseases, spaying and neutering, traveling and many other everyday activities that will involve the puppy.

The puppy, on the other hand, learns to perform on command a variety of behaviors, such as walk on a lead, sit, come, down, stand and stay. The puppy also has an opportunity to socialize with other puppies and strangers (the owners of the other puppies in the class). In other words, it learns to learn. And without ever teaching a dog how to learn, it will never be able to learn more sophisticated behaviors as an adult.

I've been teaching dog obedience classes for 25 years and have trained thousands of people and dogs. In my opinion, the dogs that have gone through KPT classes as puppies are far superior in their ability and willingness to learn and their attitude toward life and people in general than dogs that have not had that opportunity.

I have seen hundreds of puppies, which if left at home until five or six months of age before entering training classes, would have

The various forms of training an owner wishes to use will be most successful when introduced into the regimen when the puppy is at the optimum learning age. —*Don Berg*

In every litter there will be puppies that are more assertive than others. Observation will identify these and they should be placed in homes and situations where their personalities will be regarded as assets.

been shy fear-biters. But the positive experiences in KPT classes gave them the self-confidence to rise above their predisposition to shyness and become well-adjusted members of their households and communities. Their owners learned how crucial the socialization and learning processes were, and worked diligently at developing the best possible individuals they could. In addition, I have had hundreds of opportunities to observe these same puppies years later in training classes and dog activities of every conceivable kind and found their initial training was still influencing them as mature adults.

Scientific studies have proven my observations to be accurate. Researchers have found that stimulating puppies with a variety of learning experiences during this critical stage is the key to preventing the dog from becoming afraid of people and unable to cope with experiences in adulthood.

If a person were to tell me that he had the time and money to train his dog at only one stage in the puppy's life, I would not hesitate to answer, "Train him early in a KPT class. You'll find it the most rewarding experience you'll ever have with the dog and you'll never be sorry!"

Training the puppy when it is older means getting into a regular dog obedience class, also of about eight weeks duration. However, the class is likely to consist of dogs of varying ages from six months to six years and their owners. The owner will be taught how to teach his dog to walk by his side (called "heeling"), sit, stand, lie down, stay and come on command. The level of perfection expected in regular beginner's class is far different than that of a KPT class. Furthermore, there can be no socialization between the dogs since they are too old to be socially imprinted and may fight instead of socialize.

However, in spite of the fact that training an older dog is more work than training a puppy, the dogs do learn. Much of their success depends on the owner's ability to handle the dog effectively and the time he or she has to devote to practicing, as well as the dog's innate ability to learn.

Obedience classes are held in just about every town and city in the United States. The difference lies with the instructor and the method of training employed. If the instructor is knowledgeable about dog behavior and has a workable, humane method of training, the students will prosper. If the instructor has no knowledge of dog behavior and no experience (or all negative experiences) then his or her program will not be as successful regardless of the method.

The program should be successful for a majority of people attending the classes, humane and enjoyable for both dog and owner. A person wishing to join a dog obedience class can obtain the name of such an instructor in their area by contacting the National Association of Dog Obedience Instructors, 219 26th Avenue, SW, Vero Beach, Florida 32960. This organization accepts for membership only those instructors who have passed rigid examinations to determine their knowledge and ability to humanely instruct dogs and owners without regard to individual methods. They will send you a list of NADOI endorsed instructors in your area.

You can also obtain a list of training clubs in your area by writing to the American Kennel Club. Since the AKC does not endorse certain clubs and/or instructors, it would be prudent to go to one of the training sessions of the club near you to observe their methods and talk to their students.

Specialized Training

Training dogs to perform specialized behaviors is a job for people whose expertise lies within those behaviors. Training sight hounds to lure course, beagles to run rabbits at field trials, retrievers to work water trials, conformation candidates to enter dog shows, tracking dogs to track people, working breeds to enter Schutzhund trials—these are just some of the special activities owners can become involved in with their dogs. In most cases a certain amount of basic dog obedience training is a prerequisite to further training because the owner must get control before he or she can teach the dog anything else.

The American Kennel Club and local libraries are good sources for getting names and addresses of groups interested in dog activities. In addition, the national breed club (every registerable breed has one) can tell you what's going on within your own breed as far as activities are concerned. You can obtain the address of your national breed club from the American Kennel Club.

9

In the Final Analysis

$\mathbf{A}$BOUT A YEAR AGO, I sat down one day and listed 34 dogs and owners I personally knew in the United States and Australia. The criteria I used for including the dogs on my list was that I had to know them and consider them, from observations, to be good companions to their owners.

I then formulated a questionnaire that I felt would help me try to unlock the secret of why each of these dogs was a good companion to its owner. In other words, I was looking for a common denominator that ran between them all in an effort to share that secret with my readers.

The results were very interesting, considering that my poll covered a wide geographical area with a variety of lifestyles and a healthy sampling of 19 breeds, both sexes, all ages, all of whom lived in close association with their owners.

Thirty percent of the dogs were from the working and herding breeds, 30 percent were sporting dogs, and the remainder came from non-sporting, toy, terrier and hound groups. Fifty percent of the dogs were linebred while almost 50 percent were outcrossed and only one dog was inbred.

Thirty-two of the 34 dogs were acquired, not bred by their owners, and 29 of them were acquired between the ages of five and 12 weeks of age. Fifteen of the dogs lived with adults only, 16 lived with families with children and three lived with single adults.

Among the dogs there were American Kennel Club titles ranging from field and breed champions to obedience title holders such as Companion Dog, Utility Dog and Tracking Dog. One, a German Shepherd Dog, earned all of his Canadian, American and European titles, a feat no other dog has accomplished since. In contrast to this, there were more than a few dogs in the poll who were merely house pets yet they also managed to earn a rating of 10 to the question, "On a scale of 1 to 10, give your evaluation of your pet as a companion to you."

Despite the range of variation in breeds and accomplishments, there were three pieces of data that perhaps explain why each of them was, in fact, a good companion dog.

1. All the dogs had been socialized by the owner from the time they were acquired. Even the five dogs that had been acquired when they were older had been socialized by their breeders when they were puppies.
2. All the dogs had been trained in at least a Kindergarten Puppy Training or basic obedience class.
3. Sixty-five percent had been started in training before they were 20 weeks old, 25 percent had begun between the ages 20 and 52 weeks, and 10 percent had been trained after they were one year of age.

I realize how infinitesimal a group of 34 dogs is compared to the millions of dogs in the civilized world. However, something in those figures tells me they're not that far off the mark. Perhaps it's my years of training people and dogs. Perhaps it's the thousands of dogs I've watched grow up and develop. Perhaps it's the hundreds I've known that were euthanized because somewhere along the line man botched up the job and the only hope for peace for the animals was permanent sleep.

What this little study suggests is that dogs can be good companions, learn to obey, demonstrate mannerly behavior in and out of the home toward all people and function happily within the framework of the families with whom they live. It hints that socializing from an early age, beginning some type of formal training before the puppy is five months old, and making the puppy a participating member of the home community are the secrets to developing the best each puppy is capable of giving to you and your family, his pack.

Conclusion

Throughout this book, we've focused on only one theme: What it is that makes puppies the dogs they become. Through scientific research and practical experience, man has learned that there are a multitude of factors that influence the outcome of a puppy from preconception to mature adult.

We've also learned that man is (and probably always will be) the salient factor in determining the kind of dog he brings into his home as a full-time companion. From planning the breeding to final schooling, man is responsible for creating it all. And what's more, the mature dog will continue to grow and change all its life—mostly according to its man-made environment.

A large portion of what the puppy will become depends on you, the owner. Going back to that factory we mentioned in Chapter 1, the plant can make the best possible parts, but how you use them will determine the quality of the final product. You can build a shack or a mansion. But let's remember you'll have to live with it once you finish it. Happy building!

This German Shepherd Dog puppy was bred with attention to the details of breed traits, genetic history, careful rearing and the breeder's deep concern for its future. It will more than likely grow up to resemble its handsome sire.
—*Charlotte Schwartz*

166

Breeds of Dogs

THE FOLLOWING BREEDS of dogs are accepted for registration by the American Kennel Club.

SPORTING—Generally happy, active dogs that like people and other dogs. Need lots of outdoor exercise. Good with children.

Pointers—Brittany, German Shorthaired, German Wirehaired Pointer, Vizsla, Weimaraner, Wirehaired Pointing Griffon
Retrievers—Chesapeake Bay, Curly-Coated, Flat-Coated, Golden, Labrador
Setters—English, Gordon, Irish
Spaniels—American Water, Clumber, Cocker, English Cocker, English Springer, Field, Irish Water, Sussex, Welsh Springer

HOUND—Generally gentle, calm, not prone to fighting. Most are good with children.

Afghan
Basenji
Basset
Beagle
Black and Tan Coonhound
Bloodhound
Borzoi
Dachshund
Fox, American
Fox, English

Greyhound
Harrier
Ibizan
Irish Wolfhound
Norwegian Elkhound
Otter
Pharaoh
Rhodesian Ridgeback
Saluki
Scottish Deerhound
Whippet

WORKING—Generally serious, devoted to owner and family, suspicious of strangers. Need training. Eager to work for owner. Protective.

Akita
Alaskan Malamute
Bernese Mountain Dog
Boxer
Bullmastiff
Doberman Pinscher
Giant Schnauzer
Great Dane
Great Pyrenees

Komondor
Kuvasz
Mastiff
Newfoundland
Portuguese Water Dog
Rottweiler
Samoyed
Siberian Husky
Standard Schnauzer

TERRIER—Generally lively, active, vocal. Most devoted to family.

Airedale
American Staffordshire
Australian
Bedlington
Border
Bull
Cairn
Dandie Dinmont
Irish
Kerry Blue
Lakeland
Manchester (Standard)

Miniature Schnauzer
Norfolk
Norwich
Scottish
Sealyham
Skye
Smooth Fox
Soft-Coated Wheaten
Staffordshire Bull
Welsh
West Highland White
Wire Fox

TOY—Generally affectionate, people oriented. Due to size caution must be exercised around children.

Affenpinscher
Brussels Griffon
Chihuahua
English Toy
Italian Greyhound
Japanese Chin
Maltese
Manchester Terrier (Toy)

Miniature Pinscher
Papillon
Pekingese
Pomeranian
Poodle (Toy)
Pug
Shih Tzu
Silky
Yorkshire

NONSPORTING—A mixed bag. Some are good family pets, others prefer one or two adults. Most good alarm dogs.

Bichon Frise	Keeshond
Boston Terrier	Lhasa Apso
Bulldog	Miniature Poodle
Chow Chow	Schipperke
Dalmatian	Standard Poodle
French Bulldog	Tibetan Spaniel
	Tibetan Terrier

HERDING—Same as Working dogs, all instinctively herd children, adults, other pets. Protective.

Australian Cattle Dog	Collie
Bearded Collie	German Shepherd Dog
Belgian Malinois	Old English Sheepdog
Belgian Sheepdog	Puli
Belgian Tervuren	Shetland Sheepdog
Bouvier des Flandres	Welsh Corgi (Cardigan)
Briard	Welsh Corgi (Pembroke)

Note: In many breeds there are a variety of types, such as in Dachshunds. One can find longhaired, smooth, wirehaired coat types and both miniature and standard sizes. *The Complete Dog Book*, by the American Kennel Club, defines all the breeds and varieties acceptable for registration in the United States.

Bibliography

Benjamin, Carol Lea. *Mother Knows Best—The Natural Way to Train Your Dog.* Howell Book House Inc., 1985.

Bergman, Göran. *Why Does Your Dog Do That?* Howell Book House Inc., 1971.

Campbell, William E. *Behavior Problems in Dogs.* American Veterinary Publications, Inc., 1985.

Carlson, Delbert G., DVM and Giffin, James M., MD. *Dog Owner's Home Veterinary Handbook.* Howell Book House Inc., 1980.

Collins, Donald R., DVM. *The Collins Guide to Dog Nutrition.* Howell Book House Inc., 1987.

Fox, Michael W., Ph.D., DVM. *Understanding Your Dog.* Coward, McCann & Geoghegan, Inc., 1972.

Hutt, Frederick B. *Genetics for Dog Breeders.* W.H. Freeman & Co., 1979.

Mech, L. David. *The Wolf.* The Natural History Press, 1970.

Monks of New Skete. *How to Be Your Dog's Best Friend.* Little, Brown & Co.

_____. *You and Your Puppy.* Iams Food Co., 1982.

Onstott, Philip. *The New Art of Breeding Better Dogs.* Howell Book House Inc., 1983.

Pfaffenberger, Clarence J. *The New Knowledge of Dog Behavior.* Howell Book House Inc., 1963.

Prine, Virginia Bender. *How Puppies Are Born.* Howell Book House Inc., 1972.

Riser, Wayne H., DVM. *The Dog: His Varied Biological Makeup and Its Relationship to Orthopaedic Diseases.* American Animal Hospital Association & Alpo Pet Foods, Inc., 1985.

Sawyer, Braxton B. *How the New Knowledge of Genetics Can Help Breed Better Dogs.* Unpublished paper.

Scott, John Paul and Fuller, John L. *Genetics and the Social Behavior of the Dog.* University of Chicago Press, 1965.

Seranne, Ann. *The Joy of Breeding Your Own Show Dog.* Howell Book House Inc., 1984.

Trumler, Eberhard. *Understanding Your Dog.* Faber & Faber, London, England.

Vollmer, Peter J. *Puppy Rearing.* Hill's Division, Riviana Foods, 1978.

White, Kay. *Dogs: Their Mating, Whelping and Weaning.* K-R Books Ltd., Leicester, England, 1977.

Whitney, Leon F., DVM. *How to Breed Dogs.* Howell Book House, 1971.

_____. *Dog Psychology: The Basis of Dog Training.* Howell Book House, 1971.

PUPPY DEVELOPMENT CHART

By Charlotte Schwartz

DEVELOPMENT	NEONATAL PERIOD 0–12 Days	TRANSITION PERIOD 13–20 Days
BRAIN	Only partly developed. Heartbeat, balance and breathing developed. Temperature regulation/metabolism not fully developed. Poor pain reflex. Sleep center not developed.	Temperature/metabolism not yet mature. Little observable change; however, greatest maturational changes in basic capacities. Greatest change at 18–19 days.
BEHAVIORS	Activated sleep develops muscles. Sleeps in dog pile for heat. Investigative behavior based on touch and temperature only. Strongest relationship with dam—care giving. Kneads with front paws.	Interaction with dam more complex—forms social relationship with her. Shows startle response to sound—20 days. Stands—18 to 22 days. Crawls backward as well as forward. Develops lapping behavior.
MUSCLES	Forelimbs only—crawls. Hindquarters poor. Vocal chords not mature.	Eyes open at ten to 14 days, sees light/dark. Tailwagging begins at 18 to 20 days. Sucking muscles strengthen.

172

Puppy Development Chart

LITTER SOCIALIZATION PERIOD 21–35 Days	HUMAN SOCIALIZATION PERIOD Weeks 5 to 12	JUVENILE PERIOD 12 Weeks to 6 Months
Temperature/ metabolism mature at three weeks. Brain quite developed by 21 days. Cerebral cortex— vision—by 21 days. Conscious perception and control of movement. Visual and auditory perception by 28 days. Conscious sensitivity to pain. Becomes aware of environment.	Brain fully developed by five to six weeks. Memory and learning mature by end of seven weeks. Sleep center activated. Localization begins at six to seven weeks. Develops emotional reactions at six to seven weeks.	Emotional maturity begins at 13 to 16 weeks. Sexual development begins at 16 weeks to adulthood.
Head-shaking, chasing, prey killing begins at four to five weeks. Leaves nest to evacuate. Investigative and agonistic behavior begins. Sleeps in rows, not pile. Uses paws. Pack grouping begins at 28 days. Begins to mouth and chew on littermates. Mother ceases constant care.	Reacts to environmental stimuli at six to seven weeks. Extreme vocalization when left alone at six to seven weeks. Initiates social relationships with other dogs and people. Stays awake longer, sleeps apart from littermates. Explores environment from four to 12 weeks and after. Begins to carry objects. Play fighting begins. Group activities increase at five to seven weeks. Licking of dam and humans for care-giving. Dam stops producing milk at seven to 10 weeks.	Develops dominant/submissive relationships between 11 and 15 weeks. Develops avoidance response to fearful things—escape reflex. Most breeds friendly, providing they aren't afraid, up to 15 weeks. Amount of attraction to humans established by now. Male urine marking/leg lifting at five to eight months, ground scratching after that.
Leg muscles stronger, can walk, stand, run and back up. Vocal chords mature. Retina completely formed by 28 days, sees forms.	Expression, facial muscles and lips fully developed. Tail wagging fully developed, initiates social relationships.	Motor skills gain strength. Complete physical development by age two years, later for some breeds.

Puppy Development Chart

DEVELOPMENT	NEONATAL PERIOD 0–12 Days	TRANSITION PERIOD 13–20 Days
NERVES	Only some facial nerves developed. Tactile and temperature sensory developed—can distinguish between hot/cold, soft/hard. Scent not fully developed. Taste sense present. No sight, no hearing.	Sensory nerves—tactile, scent, temperature— same as Neonatal stage.
BODY CHANGES	Eyes, ears closed, eyes open approx. ten to 14 days, but don't focus well. Head swings side to side, beginning of investigatory behavior.	Reorganization of behavior, litter/dam socialization. Suffers psychologically in Transition stage if owner does not understand and act on the extreme changes taking place as puppy transforms from helpless to adult behaviors.
NEEDS	Nourishment, sleep, warmth, massage. Limited intellectual, motor capacities. Suffers physiologically in Neonatal stage by adverse environmental conditions.	Begins primary social relationships. Same physical needs as in Neonatal stage.
MEANING TO OWNER	Puppies are helpless. Dam provides all care. Owner assures dry, warm, safe environment.	Same as in Neonatal Period. Owner must provide an optimum environment for dam and puppies during period of profound changes.

NOTE: Both breed and heredity affect the social relationships of a puppy with dogs and humans. These relationships together with the environment create the individuality of a puppy. The time frames herein are average and many breeds and individuals within breeds can develop at varying times which may be perfectly normal for those individuals.

Puppy Development Chart

LITTER SOCIALIZATION PERIOD 21–35 Days	HUMAN SOCIALIZATION PERIOD Weeks 5 to 12	JUVENILE PERIOD 12 Weeks to 6 Months
Voluntary movements mature. Nerves and muscles of eliminative behavior develop—21 days, leave nest to evacuate. Sensory nerves mature at 21 days.	Nerves reach maturity, system is like adult for vision by seven to eight weeks. Fear period—eight weeks.	All sense organs developed by approx. 12 weeks. Another fear period.
Can eat semi-liquid food. Can hear and see respond to stimuli. First teeth appear in gums.	Elongation of muzzle. Body begins to take on shape of adults. Begins to chew solid food.	Permanent teeth begin to emerge at 16 weeks. Bitches come into first estrus at five to eight months. Male testicles stay in the scrotum permanently at seven to 12 months. Complete pattern of adult sexual behavior marks end of Juvenile stage.
Needs social interaction with littermates. Limited human contact. Unaltered environment. Week four critical—dam begins to stand while nursing, vomits to introduce pups to semi-liquid diet. Optimum learning time begins.	Needs personal attention from humans away from littermates and dam. Needs social play—humans. Puppy Testing 6½ to 7½ weeks. Needs to understand and accept human dominance. Needs to begin KPT class. Has short attention span. Susceptible to psychological damage now.	Latest opportunity to remove puppy from dam and litter without it becoming too dependent on dogs for social pack. Remove from litter by 12 weeks. Needs experiences in the outside world before 12 weeks. Training should continue.
Dam gradually reduces care. Owner begins limited handling of puppies.	Dam's role is one of pack leader, teacher. Owner assumes care-giving role. Must interact in social and dominant role and provide new experiences and permanent home. Must aid puppy's psychological and physical growth.	Puppy becomes an independent organism. Owner gives all care and learning experiences for complete development of puppy.